SCHOL

The Best of **NURSERY** education

# Creative play

## Ages 3-5

▶ **Outdoor play ideas**
▶ **Songs to familiar tunes**
▶ **Cookery activities**
▶ **Display ideas**

**All the best activities from the UK's leading early years magazine**

**Editor**
Susan Elliott

**Designers**
Andrea Lewis and Joy Monkhouse

**Cover photograph**
Ray Moller

Acknowledgement
Qualifications and Curriculum Authority for the use of extracts from the QCA/
DfEE document Curriculum Guidance for the Foundation Stage © 2000
Qualification and Curriculum Authority.

© 2005, Scholastic Ltd

Published by Scholastic Ltd, Villiers House,
Clarendon Avenue, Leamington Spa, Warwickshire CV32 5PR.

Visit our website at www.scholastic.co.uk

Printed in Singapore.

2 3 4 5 6 7 8 9 0   6 7 8 9 0 1 2 3 4

**British Library Cataloguing-in-Publication Data.** A catalogue record for
this book is available from the British Library.

**ISBN 0-439-96508-X**
**ISBN 9-780-439-96508-8**

All articles previously published in *Nursery Education* magazine between
September 2001and June 2004.

# Contents

# Foreword

**By Sue Owen, Director, Early Childhood Unit, National Children's Bureau.**

Even the most well qualified, experienced and creative of professionals need a few fresh ideas from time to time.

Most early years practitioners take inspiration from the practical projects and themes provided, in abundance, by magazines aimed at our sector, and *Nursery Education's* are among the best.

A recent study on how early years practitioners access information, conducted by the National Children's Bureau, found that the majority of respondents relied on magazines for up-dates and tips as well as on their colleagues.

This series helpfully pulls together a collection of *Nursery Education's* projects, so you can find them all in one place.

Often the best ideas and projects arise out of children's own interests – many of which are reflected in this collection. The collection offers new ideas (and reminders for some trusted favourites which you may have forgotten) as springboards for your work.

Resources such as this are an ideal addition to team discussions. They can stimulate new thinking as well as bringing the knowledge of a wide range of early years experts to the table.

Thanks to *Nursery Education's* new resource collection, practitioners will now have access to a pool of information from colleagues across the country.

# Introduction

If you're a regular subscriber to *Nursery Education*, you'll already appreciate just what a versatile, time-saving resource the magazine is. Each issue contains all you need to deliver a themed project in your setting, plus essential information that enables you to keep up-to-date with current developments in the early years sector.

We've built on this successful formula and made it even better by selecting the very best activities and information from past issues of the magazine, and compiling them into a series of exciting new books.

Each title is packed full of original ideas that are guaranteed to enthuse your children and inspire your staff. This book contains a selection of creative play activities that will help the children to develop a range of skills across the curriculum. From exciting outdoor play ideas and fun recipes to stunning displays and lively songs, these activities will help you to make the most of the space available in and around your setting.

We've had great fun putting this new set of books together, and we hope you find them to be a valuable addition to your setting! If you would like more information on *Nursery Education*, please visit our website www.scholastic.co.uk, telephone: 0845 850 4411 or see page 64 of this book.

**Sarah Sodhi,** Editor,
*Nursery Education* magazine.

# Chapter 1
# Outdoor play

Whatever the size of your outdoor area, you'll find the inspiration for lots of fun outdoor learning in this chapter. From games and races to role-play and art, these activities will help to develop a range of skills across the curriculum.

# Run rabbit, run!

**Focus on spatial awareness with these fun activities based on running rabbits**

## Rabbit runs

**Stepping Stone:** negotiate appropriate pathways when walking or running outdoors (PD).
**Early learning Goal:** show awareness of space, of themselves and of others (PD).
**Group size:** eight to ten children.

### What you need

Outdoor play space, free from obstructions; bright carpet square or marker for each child.

### What to do

● Begin by talking about the children's pets. Does anyone have a rabbit? What is it called? How does it move? Invite the child to demonstrate how their pet moves to the rest of the group.
● Explain that pet rabbits normally live in hutches outdoors, and some have rabbit runs to give them even more space.
● Take the children outdoors and explain about safety outdoors. Define the boundaries.
● Invite the children to take a marker or carpet square. Ask them to put the marker on a space on the ground and stand on it. Make sure that the markers are well spaced so that the children can walk between them.
● Explain that the children are going to pretend to be rabbits. The marker is their hutch and the space between the markers is the rabbit run. Tell them that rabbits venture out to nibble grass or to explore but go back to their hutch when they are hungry or sense danger.
● Invite the children move in and out of the markers without touching them. Remind them to move safely without bumping into one another.

© Photo Disc Inc.

● When you call out 'Run rabbit, run!', the children should run back to their own hutches.
● Repeat several times, then reposition the 'hutches' to make the activity more challenging.

### Support and extension

For younger children, choose larger markers and place them further apart. Let them play the game individually or follow another child. Encourage older, more able children to bunny hop like rabbits. Move the markers closer together to make the activity more challenging.

## Bedtime for bunnies

**Stepping Stone:** show respect for other children's space when playing among them (PD).
**Early learning Goal:** show awareness of space, of themselves and of others (PD).
**Group size:** eight to ten children.

### What you need

Grassed outdoor space, free from obstructions: large blanket.

### What to do

● Spread the blanket on the ground and invite the children to sit on it. Explain to them that it is the rabbit's home.
● Encourage the children to be baby bunnies exploring their new hutch. Tell them to move carefully around the blanket without touching each other or the grass.
● Invite the children to move off the blanket to explore the outdoor space. Call out 'Bedtime for bunnies!' as the signal for the children to come back. Remind them to stay on the blanket and to move safely without bumping into one another.
● Explain that baby bunnies need gentle handling and lots of sleep. Let the children hide underneath the blanket when it is bedtime for bunnies.

### Support and extension

Let younger children sit on the blanket with an adult to watch the activity. Invite them to imitate and follow other more confident children. Older children can lead the free exploration of the outdoor space.

## Home links

● Encourage the children to look for pictures of bunnies in their story-books at home.
● Collect recyclable materials to create pet play homes.

## Further idea

● Make the 'Rabbit runs' activity more exciting by whispering or shouting the word 'Fox!' unexpectedly as the signal for the rabbits to return home.

**Janice Filer** is an early years practitioner and author.

# Ribbons and races

**Enjoy using your outdoor area to make shapes on a large scale**

## Moving circles
**Stepping Stone:** show curiosity and observation by talking about shapes, how they are the same or why some are different (MD).
**Early Learning Goal:** talk about, recognise and recreate simple patterns (MD).
**Group size:** ten to 15 children.

### What you need
A metre length of ribbon for each child; hoops and quoits; large outdoor space.

### What to do
● Give each child a length of ribbon and ask them to find a safe space to stand where they cannot touch anyone else.
● Ask the children to hold one end of the ribbon tightly and wave it as high as they can, then as low as they can.
● Show them the hoops and quoits and talk about circle shapes. Encourage the children to make a large circular movement by twirling their ribbons in the air.
● Make big then little circle shapes. Talk with the children about the way that the ribbons move.
● Next, ask the children to curl up the ribbon on the ground to make a circle. Let everyone walk, then hop, run and skip around their own circle.
● Now ask the children to get into groups of threes and lay all their ribbons together, end to end, to make one big circle. Encourage them to dance around the circle, chanting 'Round the circle we go'.
● Let two groups join together to make a bigger circle and repeat the activity.

● Finally, invite all the children to put their lengths of ribbon together to make the biggest circle possible.

### Support and extension
Chalk circle shapes on the ground as a guide for younger children. Let older children join their ribbons together to make triangles, squares and rectangles of different sizes.

© Hilda Offen

**Home links**
● Send home shape cards and ask parents to play the 'Shape stations' game at home with their children.

## Shape stations
**Stepping Stone:** match some shapes by recognising similarities and orientation (MD).
**Early Learning Goal:** use language such as 'circle' or 'bigger' to describe the shape and size of solids and flat shapes (MD).
**Group size:** ten children.

### What you need
Four large shape cards (circle, triangle, square, rectangle); smaller matching cards; sticky tape; tambourine; chalk.

### What to do
● Chalk different shapes on the ground, or space out the large shape cards around the area.
● Tap the tambourine and chant the word 'circle'. Encourage the children to try to walk in a circle in their own space, without touching anyone else.

When you stop tapping the tambourine, the children should run to the nearest circle shape.
● Repeat the activity, chanting 'triangle', then 'square' and so on, encouraging the children to try to recreate the shape each time. Vary the movements and sizes by chanting, for example, 'big square' or 'small rectangle'.
● Now tape the cards to the wall.
● This time, when you stop playing, hold up one of the smaller shape cards. The children should run and stand by the matching wall sign as you display each shape card in turn.
● Play several times, then add an extra challenge by playing 'last one there is out'.

### Support and extension
Call out the names of the shapes for younger children and point to the correct sign. For older children, write the words on the shapes.

**Further idea**
● Play 'Shape I spy' trying to find as many different shapes as possible around your setting.

**Pauline Kenyon** is Senior Primary Inspector for Dudley LEA.

# Busy buzzy bees!

**Enjoy these fun activities inspired by the movements and habits of bumble-bees**

## Beeline dance

**Stepping Stone:** relate and make attachments to members of their group (PSED).
**Early Learning Goal:** work as part of a group, taking turns (PSED).
**Group size:** ten children.

### What you need
Six cones; access to an outdoor area; additional adult help.

### What to do
● On a warm summer's day, go outdoors and look for bees.
● Encourage the children to look carefully at flowers where the bees are feeding and to watch them move as they buzz from flower to flower.
● Talk about a bee's furry body, its colour and how its wings buzz as it flies. Remind the children that bees can sting and that they should not get too close.
● Invite the children to make up a bee dance. Form a line, one behind the other. Encourage the child at the front to start the dance, or join the front of the line yourself. Pretend to buzz around like bees, adding appropriate sound effects!
● Now set up the cones in a line with plenty of space in between. Invite the line of buzzy bees to weave in and out of the cones, following the actions of the child at the front.
● Make sure that each child has a turn at leading the line.

### Support and extension
If younger children find it difficult to stay in line, let them practise dancing and moving around the outdoor area independently, until they feel safe and secure enough to join in with the rest of the group. Provide more cones as obstacles to challenge older children and encourage them to move fast or slow on command.

### Home links
● Ask parents to contribute towards an interest table all about bees. Suggest items such as jars of honey, pictures or books, beeswax polish and soft toys.

© Stockbyte

## Flower power

**Stepping Stone:** move freely with pleasure and confidence (PD).
**Early Learning Goal:** move with confidence, imagination and in safety (PD).
**Group size:** ten children.

### What you need
A4 card in a variety of colours; pens; scissors; sticky tape; outdoor space.

### What to do
● Remind the children about the bees that you saw visiting the flowers. What were they doing on the flowers? How did they travel between them?
● Explain that you want them to pretend to be bees feeding from large flowers.

● Invite the children to draw and cut out flower shapes from the A4 card. Randomly stick the flowers around your outdoor area.
● Encourage the children to experiment with different ways of moving as they visit each flower. Place some flowers out of the children's reach so that they have to jump up to touch them, and others low to encourage the children to bend and crouch down.
● Challenge the children to touch as many flowers as they can using different ways of moving between them.

### Support and extension
Plan time for younger children to use the outdoor area in small groups so that they explore their own potential and gain confidence. Encourage older children to visit different-coloured flowers in the order in which you name them.

### Further ideas
● Over the space of a week, hunt for minibeasts outdoors. Compile a record to see which is the most common.

● Enhance your movement activities by playing suitable music such as Rimsky-Korsakov's Flight of the Bumblebee.

**Lorraine Frankish** is an early years tutor and NVQ assessor.

# Catch of the day!

**Get messy with these physical activities for your outdoor area**

## Watery wonderwall

**Stepping Stone:** explore what happens when they to mix colours (CD).
**Early Learning Goal:** explore colour, texture, shape, form and space in two or three dimensions (CD).
**Group size:** eight children.

### What you need
Watered-down poster or powder paints in a variety of blues and greens; spray bottles; roll of paper; drawing pins or sticky tape; aprons.

### What to do
● This is a perfect outdoor activity as it requires a lot of space and gives the children the freedom to be messy. The finished mural makes a lovely display.
● Fix a long roll of paper to a fence or wall with drawing pins or sticky tape.
● Fill the spray bottles with thin watered-down powder or poster paint in a variety of blues and greens.
● Show the children how to squirt the paint on to the paper, then give them a free hand to spray the paint on to the paper to create an underwater effect.
● As the colours begin to run and overlap together on the paper, discuss the way that they are mixing and changing.

### Support and extension
Let younger children splash the colour on using a large decorator's brush. When the mural is dry, invite older children to paint fish on it.

© Angela Lambert

## Home links
● Ask parents to share books or photographs showing fish or the sea with their children at home.

● Find out whether the children eat fish at home and discuss tastes, smells and textures.

## Further ideas
● Add drops of paint to a tray of water. Observe how the paint dissolves and changes the colour of water.

● Discuss the dangers of water and how to stay safe.

● Take the children to look at a fish counter in a supermarket.

● Visit a pet shop with aquariums so that the children can observe live fish.

## Catching fish

**Stepping Stone:** negotiate space successfully when playing racing and chasing games (PD).
**Early Learning Goal:** move with confidence, imagination and in safety (PD).
**Group size:** eight children.

### What you need
Outdoor space; fishing nets and rods, if available.

### What to do
● Talk about how fish are caught in the sea. What do fishermen use to catch fish? Talk about fishing nets and rods and if possible, show the children examples.
● Tell the children that they are going to play a chasing game to catch some 'fish'!
● Invite one child to be a fisherman and the other children to be the fish. Encourage the fish to move around the outdoor area. The fisherman has to catch a fish by touching a child's shoulder.
● The fisherman and fish then join hands and continue to catch the other fish. Each time that a fish is caught, they join hands to make the 'fishing net' bigger.
● Continue playing the game until all of the fish have been caught. The last child to be caught becomes the fisherman for the next game.

### Support and extension
Make the game easier for younger children by being the fisherman yourself and limiting the size of the 'net' to no more than three children. Call out commands for older children, such as 'rough sea' (move quickly), 'calm sea' (move slowly) or 'shark coming' (run and hide)!

**Lorraine Frankish**
is an early years tutor and NVQ assessor.

# Ticket to travel

**Enjoy an imaginary trip around the world with these lively play ideas**

## Off we go

**Stepping Stones:** use available resources to create props for role-play; play alongside other children engaged in the same theme (CD).

**Early Learning Goal:** use their imagination in role-play (CD).

**Group size:** up to six children.

## What you need

Large cardboard boxes; large wooden bricks; play tent; rucksacks; old passport; sleeping-bag or blanket; maps; torch; holiday brochures; card; pens; scissors; notebooks; inkpad and stamp; chalks.

© Estelle Corke

## What to do

● Look at the maps and holiday brochures together. Talk about travelling around the world and choose some resorts or countries that you would like to visit!

● Show the children the passport and talk about buying tickets. Ask if anyone has ever travelled in an aeroplane.

● Make some pretend travel tickets and passports. Put up the tent and pack the rucksack together. Help the children to make a ticket office and an aeroplane from the large boxes and wooden bricks.

● Mark some destinations on the ground with chalks.

● Play alongside the children travelling on the aeroplane, buying tickets and staying in the tent. Use the children's own ideas of places to visit.

● Comment on what you see is happening and ask open questions to encourage the children to listen to each other's ideas and to play together co-operatively.

## Support and extension

Join in with younger children, modelling simple pretend play such as buying a ticket or stamping the pretend passports. Encourage older children to find mountains and the sea on the maps.

## Home links

● Invite parents to mark friends' and families' homes on the world map.

## In my tent

**Stepping Stone:** show increasing control over clothing and fastenings (PD).

**Early Learning Goal:** move with control and co-ordination (PD).

**Group size:** up to six children.

### What you need

Holiday brochures; box of dressing-up clothes; small table; hoop; pens and card for pretend tickets; rucksack; blanket; play tent.

### What to do

● Set up a world traveller obstacle course. Challenge the first child to jump to the box of dressing-up clothes.

● When they reach the box, encourage them to put on an item of clothing, and then move in another way, such as hopping or skipping, to the ticket desk.

● At the ticket desk, help each child to write a ticket using the pens and card and to put it in their pocket.

● Encourage them to crawl through the hoop and under the blanket. When they have emerged from the other side of the blanket, ask them to take off the dressing-up clothes and put them in the rucksack. Take care with the rucksack fasteners.

● The child should then go into the tent and drop the rucksack to end their journey.

● Empty the rucksack and let the second child start the obstacle course.

### Support and extension

Shorten the obstacle course for younger children to just two items. Go down the obstacle course alongside them providing a commentary and modelling the actions for them to copy. Encourage older children to work in pairs, completing all the actions together as a team.

## Further ideas

● Look at a world map together. Find the sea and the mountains. Can the children find the United Kingdom?

● Make tickets and passports and add rucksacks, travel brochures, maps and a sleeping-bag to your home corner.

**Clare Beswick** is an early years and childcare consultant.

# Out in the country

**Have fun in the fresh air with these exciting parachute games**

## I saw a sheep

**Stepping Stone:** move body position as necessary (PD).
**Early Learning Goal:** show awareness of space, of themselves and others (PD).
**Group size:** six to eight children.

### What you need

A parachute or large sheet; small bag containing toys (or pictures), including a cow, horse, tractor, sheep, ducks, grain and birds.

### What to do

● Spread out the parachute or sheet and, with the children holding the edges, lift the sheet to the children's waist height.
● Place the bag of pictures and small toys in the middle of the ground under the parachute.
● Invite a child to go under the parachute and choose an object or picture, for example, grain.
● Using the tune of the traditional nursery song, 'I Went to Visit a Farm One Day' from *This Little Puffin...* compiled by Elizabeth Matterson (Puffin Books), sing:

*I went to visit the country one day,*
*I saw some grain across the way*
*And what do you think I heard it say?*
*Swish, swish, swish.*

● While singing the song, place the object or picture from the bag on the parachute and dance around in a circle. Encourage the children to move together, pulling the parachute taut, keeping the object in the middle of the parachute.

● Continue playing, taking turns to choose an object from the bag and adapting the song.

### Support and extension

Keep younger children close to you. Encourage older children to describe the object that they have chosen for the rest of the group to guess.

© PhotoDisc Inc.

## Home links

● Ask parents to help their child to bring in seeds from the garden, or perhaps pips or seeds from fruit.

## Oats and beans

**Stepping Stone:** show an awareness of change (KUW).
**Early Learning Goals:** look closely at similarities, differences, patterns and change (KUW).
**Group size:** eight children.

### What you need

A parachute or large sheet; number dice.

### What to do

● Spread out the sheet or parachute on the floor and ask the children to stand around it, holding the edges.
● Sing the traditional nursery song 'Oats and Beans and Barley Grow' from *This Little Puffin...* compiled by Elizabeth Matterson (Puffin Books).

● As you sing, slowly move the parachute up from the ground to as high as the children can reach.
● Next, lower the parachute slowly to the floor. Throw the dice and count the number of spots. Help a child to choose this number of seeds and to crawl under the parachute to 'plant' the seeds.
● Sing the song again and lift the parachute as high as it will go. Slowly lower the parachute, throw the dice and encourage the next child to add that number of seeds.
● Continue playing until all the children have crawled under the parachute to 'plant' some seeds.

### Support and extension

Raise the parachute a little higher to make it easier for younger children to crawl under. Ask older children to count the total number of seeds.

## Further ideas

● Look at seed heads. Observe them as they dry and then gather the seeds.

● Open up a watermelon or a pomegranate and count or weigh the seeds.

**Clare Beswick** is an early years and childcare consultant.

# Autumn leaves

**Put the fallen leaves around your setting to good use with these exciting outdoor play ideas**

## Compost heap

**Stepping Stones:** show curiosity, observe and manipulate objects and materials; describe simple features of objects and events (KUW).
**Early Learning Goals:** investigate objects and materials by using all of their senses as appropriate; find out about, and identify, some features of living things, objects and events they observe (KUW).
**Group size:** small group to set up compost bin; whole group to collect leaves.

### What you need
Compost bin; pictures of plants and gardens.

### What to do
● Talk to the children about their gardens. Who does the gardening at home? Does anyone have a compost bin? What do they put into it?
● Share the pictures and discuss the things that plants need in order to grow healthy and strong.
● Explain what compost is and how it is used to make the soil 'extra healthy' for plants. Tell the children that they are going to make some compost to use on the plants around your setting.
● Set up the compost bin in a suitable place outside.
● Encourage the children to collect leaves and seeds to put in the compost bin on a regular basis. Other garden waste and fruit and vegetable waste can also be added to the bin.
● The compost will take approximately six months to mature. During this time, encourage the children to observe and record the changes in the leaves and seeds, as well as the minibeasts that inhabit the compost. Talk about the changing texture and smells.
● In the spring, let the children add the compost to the flowerbeds in your setting.

### Support and extension
All the children should be able to take part in this activity with relative ease. Let younger children help to create an indoor garden. Invite older children to display their recordings of the changes to the compost.

### Home links
● Encourage parents to help their children collect leaves from their gardens or from walks. Make a display of the children's finds, labelling who found what and where!

© Estelle Corke

## Falling leaves

**Stepping Stone:** respond to rhythm and music, by means of gesture and movement (PD).
**Early Learning Goal:** move with confidence, imagination and in safety (PD).
**Group size:** ten to 12 children.

### What you need
CD or tape of 'Autumn' from *The Four Seasons* by Vivaldi; CD player or tape recorder that can be used outdoors; pictures of trees in each of the seasons; selection of leaves.

### What to do
● Show the children the pictures of the trees. Encourage them to point out the differences. In which season do many trees lose their leaves?
● Go outdoors and look at any surrounding trees. Show the children the collection of leaves. Hold them up high and let them fall to the ground.
● Encourage the children to describe how they fall. Introduce vocabulary such as 'swirling', 'twirling', 'spinning', 'twisting', 'whirling' and 'floating'.
● Invite the children to find a large space and pretend to be leaves falling from the trees. Encourage them to move in a variety of ways, using all of their bodies.
● Play the music and encourage the children to move in time to it.

### Support and extension
Support younger children by helping them to explore different movements. Provide obstacles for older children to practise moving around.

### Further ideas
● Blow bubbles outside and encourage the children to chase them around, or to move like the bubbles floating through the air on calm or windy days.

**Jenny Etheredge** is the Pre-School Leader at Thames Pre-School in Cricklade, Wiltshire.

Creative play

# Branching out

**Enjoy finding out about the Jewish festival of Tu B'Shevat and playing some fun outdoor games**

## Fruit salad

**Stepping Stones:** can stop; negotiate space when playing running and chasing games with other children (PD).
**Early Learning Goal:** move with confidence, imagination and safety (PD).
**Group size:** whole group.

### What you need

Information book about the festival of Tu B'Shevat; chalks.

### What to do

● Talk to the children about the Jewish festival of Tu B'Shevat using the information in the book. Explain that it is a time to celebrate trees and the fruits that grow on trees.
● Explain that many people of the Jewish faith plant new trees and eat special foods made with the fruit of trees.
● Ask the children if they can name some fruits that grow on trees.
● Draw three large apples on the ground in one corner of the outdoor play area, then three pears in the next corner, three lemons in a third corner and three oranges in a fourth corner.
● Draw a large circle in the middle to represent the salad bowl.
● Ask the children to stand in the salad bowl. Call out one of the four fruits and encourage the children to run to that area, jump on that fruit and then run back to the bowl.

● Continue playing the game, varying it by asking the children to tiptoe or use giant strides as they make their way to the fruits.

### Support and extension

Limit the group size to three for younger children. Call out two fruits at a time for the older children.

© Jenny Tulip

## Target the tree

**Stepping Stone:** use increasing control over an object by throwing or catching it (PD).
**Early Learning Goal:** use a range of small and large equipment (PD).
**Group size:** four to six children.

### What you need

Chalks; six beanbags; information book about the festival of Tu B'Shevat.

### What to do

● Begin by talking to the children about the Jewish festival of Tu B'Shevat using the information in the book.
● Ask the children to list the different parts of a tree, including the roots, trunk, branches and leaves.

● Together, draw a large tree on the ground with the chalks. Name the different parts as you draw it and encourage the children to think about how the tree grows and changes through the seasons.
● Invite each child to throw a beanbag at the tree shape. At the end of the first round, ask the children to say where their beanbag has landed. Whose beanbag is the highest up the tree? Whose is near the roots? Whose beanbag is on the trunk?
● Play the game again, this time encouraging the children to aim to land the beanbags on individual branches.

### Support and extension

Allow younger children to stand close to the tree for their throw. Throw the beanbag to older children to catch, before they have their turn throwing it.

### Home links

● Make a list of some unusual fruits and ask parents to help their children to spot them on their next shopping trip.

● Invite the children to bring a leaf to your setting so that they can make a leaf print together with their parents. Hang these leaves from a branch and encourage each child to hunt for the leaf print that they have made.

### Further ideas

● Look at and taste some fruits traditionally grown in Israel, such as figs, dates, olives and pomegranates.

● Make fruit pie with some locally -grown fruit.

**Clare Beswick** is an early years and childcare consultant.

# Under canvas

**Children love playing in tents, so make the most of this stimulating experience to explore and create your own tents outdoors**

## Let's go camping

**Stepping Stone:** engage in imaginative and role-play based on own first-hand experiences (CD).
**Early Learning Goal:** use their imagination in role-play and stories (CD).
**Group size:** four children.

### What you need

Two pop-up tents; small rucksacks; sleeping bags; picnic items such as food and flasks of cold drinks for four children; large items of nightwear; torches; large rucksack; camping holiday brochures; catalogues showing camping gear.

### What to do

● Check for any food allergies and dietary requirements.
● Discuss the children's experiences of tents and look at pictures in the catalogues and brochures.
● Talk about how tents become homes for a short while when families go on holiday. Pretend to go on a camping holiday.
● Talk about items that might be needed for an overnight stay in a tent and gather them together on a clear floor space.
● Ask each child to pack a rucksack with overnight clothes and roll up a sleeping bag. Pack the large rucksack with the food, drink and torches.

● Invite each child to carry a packed rucksack and rolled sleeping bag while you carry the large rucksack and tents.
● Go outside and choose somewhere to set up camp. Have fun putting on nightwear over clothes, eating the picnic, singing songs and settling down in sleeping bags in the tents.

### Support and extension

Set up the camp beforehand for younger children and sit in tents for a picnic. Let older children build their own tents from planks, boxes and blankets.

© Derek Cooknell

### Home links

● Suggest that parents make a tent from a clothes horse and blanket for their children to play in outdoors.

## Tepee homes

**Stepping Stone:** gain an awareness of the cultures and beliefs of others (KUW).
**Early Learning Goal:** begin to know about their own cultures and beliefs and those of other people (KUW).
**Group size:** four children.

### What you need

Six thick garden canes; wide masking tape; white sheet; paint; resources chosen by the children from home corner; pictures of tepees.

### What to do

● Talk about North American Indian tepees and look at the pictures of them. Explain that the North American Indians make their homes in tepees.

● Compare the tepees with other tents.
● Create a tepee outdoors. Fasten the garden canes together at one end with masking tape and pull them outwards at the bottom to form the frame.
● Ask the children to paint pictures and patterns on a large sheet.
● Cut a hole in the sheet, push it over the canes and let it fall around the frame. Cut a slit for a door and tuck the bottom under the canes.
● Let the children pretend to be North American Indians and choose what to put in the tepee.
● Have fun playing freely in the tepee.

### Support and extension

Create the tepee beforehand for younger children. Show older children how to use a small blanket to make a papoose in which they can carry a doll.

### Further ideas

● Find pictures of other tents such as circus tents and marquees, and discuss events that take place inside them.

● Organise a campsite outdoors for dolls using smaller garden canes and lengths of fabric to create the tents.

**Jean Evans** is an early years consultant and author

# Picture perfect

**Enjoy a treasure hunt and the freedom of painting outside with these fresh outdoor ideas**

## Go seek

**Stepping Stone:** find items from positional/directional clues (MD).
**Early Learning Goal:** use everyday words to describe position (MD).
**Group size:** four to six children per adult.

### What you need
Outdoor play equipment; individual laminated photographs of each of the children and helpers in your group.

### Preparation
● Place the outdoor play equipment safely in various locations outside of your setting.
● Without the children seeing, hide three photographs on various pieces of equipment. Make sure that the locations can all be reached safely.

### What to do
● Tell the children that you have hidden three photographs around your outdoor area.
● Explain that you would like the children to find the photographs and that you will give them some clues as to where they are and how they can be reached. For example, 'Crawl to find Sophie's picture' or 'Look behind the tunnel to find Daniel's picture'.
● Once the children have found all three photographs, give those children that found them a new photograph to hide.
● Invite the children that have hidden the photograhs to make up clues for the other children to find them.
● Continue the activity until all the children have had the opportunity to hide a photograph and make up clues.

© Derek Cooknell

### Support and extension
Provide very simple clues to help younger children to find the photographs, such as 'Have a look under the slide'. Give more detailed positional clues for older children, such as 'It is next to the slide, but behind the bench'.

**Home links**
● Encourage parents to play traditional outdoor ball games with their children, such as football, cricket or bowls.

## Look at us!

**Stepping Stone:** work creatively on a large scale (CD).
**Early Learning Goal:** explore colour, texture, shape, form and space in two or three dimensions (CD).
**Group size:** four to six children.

### What you need
A sunny day; large sheet of hardboard; ready-mixed coloured paints (thickened with PVA glue); large paintbrushes; mirrors; waterproof clear varnish; adult helpers, if possible.

### What to do
● Suggest that the children make a big picture to display outside.
● Explain that you would like each of the children to draw a big picture of themselves.
● Help the children to take turns to paint a large picture of themselves (looking in the mirror, if necessary) on to the hardboard using the thick paints and large brushes.
● Encourage the children to think of a member of their family and to paint a picture of them as well.
● Once dry, an adult should varnish the children's work.
● Display the pictures together as a frieze outside on dry days or in a play area or entrance.
● Encourage the children to show their picture to parents and visitors.

### Support and extension
Let younger children interpret their subjects as they choose. Encourage older children to use the appropriate hair and eye colours for their pictures of themselves and their family.

**Further ideas**
● Invite the children to tell you how many people live in their house.

● Call out a number and encourage the children to form groups of that number of children.

**Lorraine Gale**
is a teacher and writer.

## Outdoor play
# Bear in mind

**Let your favourite teddies take centre stage with these great outdoor activities**

## Sorting sizes

**Stepping Stone:** show curiosity and observation by talking about shapes, how they are the same or why some are different (MD).

**Early Learning Goal:** use language such as 'greater', 'smaller', 'heavier' or 'lighter' to compare quantities (MD).

**Group size:** no less than two children, and up to whole group.

### What you need

Teddy bears of varying shapes, sizes and weights; camera (optional); three hoops; card; marker pen.

### What to do

● Explain to the children that you are going to work as a team to put the teddy bears in order.

● Talk about and compare the height, shape, weight and size of the teddy bears. For example, 'Chen's teddy is really tiny, it reminds me of Baby Bear in the story of "Goldilocks and the Three Bears"! Does anyone have a medium-sized mummy bear or a daddy-sized big bear?'.

● Encourage the children to group themselves into small, medium and large teddy bear groups.

● Challenge the children to form a line in order of size and, if possible, take a photograph.

● Let the children sit their teddy bears on the ground 'for a rest' and encourage them to come to look at the size line from the front, seeing how the bears get smaller and shorter, and from the back, observing them get taller or bigger.

● Place three hoops on the floor and put the cards with the words 'small', 'medium' and 'large' inside the hoops.

● Invite the children to play a game of 'Tag'. Each time that they are caught, they must place their teddy into the hoop that best describes its size.

### Support and extension

Talk younger children through their decision-making process. Invite older children to work independently to sort the teddy bears into the hoops.

© Derek Cooknell / Jigsaw Nursery

### Home links

● Write a diary of Teddy's adventures.

● Invite parents and grandparents to come in and talk about their teddy bears, how old they are, their names and where they came from.

## Lost and found

**Stepping Stone:** relate and make attachments to members of their group (PSED).

**Early Learning Goal:** work as part of a group or class, taking turns and sharing fairly (PSED).

**Group size:** whole group.

### What you need

Teddy bear; story about a teddy bear, such as *Lost on the Beach* by Ian Beck (Scholastic).

### What to do

● Share the story with the children and invite them to sit in a circle with you.

● Explain that you are going to hide a teddy bear behind one child in the group.

● Ask one volunteer to sit in the centre of the circle and close their eyes, while the rest of the group watch you hide the teddy.

● Gently lean the teddy against the back of one child and encourage the children to sit with their hands in front of them and keep it a secret.

● Ask the child in the middle to open their eyes and encourage everyone to sing, to the tune of 'The Wheels on the Bus':

*Teddy bear, teddy bear, where are you?*
*Teddy bear, teddy bear, where are you?*
*Teddy bear, teddy bear, where are you?*
*Where are you hiding?*

● Invite the child in the middle to crawl on their hands and knees around the circle to each child that they think may be hiding the teddy, while the rest of the children hum the tune.

● If the child is close to finding the teddy, encourage the children to hum very loudly, but if the child is away from it, they must hum softly.

● Congratulate the child when they find the teddy bear and repeat the activity with the rest of the group.

### Support and extension

Move around the circle with younger children, helping to keep them focused. Challenge older children to hide the teddy bear among themselves and lead the humming.

### Further ideas

● Have a 'teddy bear race' with the children running a race holding their teddies. Position them 1st, 2nd, 3rd, 4th and so on, ensuring that everyone receives a prize.

**Martine Horvath** is a Reception teacher and early years educational consultant.

Creative play

# Giant fun and games

**Make the most of your outdoor space with these exciting movement activities**

## Here comes Daisy!

**Stepping Stone:** combine and repeat a range of movements (PD).
**Early Learning Goal:** move with control and co-ordination (PD).
**Group size:** five to 15 children.

### What you need

Large open space.

### What to do

● Sit together in a circle and talk about the different characters in the story of 'Jack and the Beanstalk'.
● Encourage the children to name each character, then move around the space in the manner of each character.
● Ask everyone to sit down again, and introduce the following chant:

*Are you walking, walking, walking?*
*Hear Jack's footsteps walking.*
*Are you plodding, plodding, plodding?*
*Hear Daisy's footsteps plodding.*
*Are you running, running, running?*
*Hear the giant's footsteps running.*

● When the children are familiar with the chant, stand up and say it again, this time changing your style of movement as you chant the words for each character.
● Make up some extra lines for the verse for the sounds and movements of the goose, the harp and Jack's mother.

© Gaynor Berry

### Support and extension

Encourage younger children to get on their hands and knees when they are being Daisy, and to stretch up tall for the giant. Challenge older children to add extra verses incorporating outdoor equipment, such as your climbing frame or slide.

## Don't wake the giant

**Stepping Stones:** can stop; negotiate space successfully when playing racing and chasing games with other children (PD).
**Early Learning Goal:** move with confidence, imagination and in safety (PD).
**Group size:** three to ten children.

### What you need

Large open space; simple drawing of the giant's face (A5 size); thin card; glue; colouring materials; soft toy or plastic goose. (Alternatively, make your own by cutting two goose shapes from yellow felt and gluing them together. Stuff the goose with scrap fabric or crumpled-up newspaper.)

### What to do

● Tell the children that they are going to play a game to try to steal the giant's magic goose!
● Invite them to colour in the giant's face. Laminate it and cut around the outline then stick it on to a strip of card. Bend and glue the card to make a child-sized headband.
● Invite a child to be the giant and to wear the headband. The giant should stand at one end of the space with his back to the group.
● Place the goose just behind the giant.
● Play a version of 'Grandmother's Footsteps', encouraging the children to pretend to be Jack, creeping up behind the giant to steal the magic goose. If the giant wakes up, turns around and sees anyone moving, they have to go back to the beginning.
● When someone manages to take the goose, let them swap places with the giant, then play again.

### Support and extension

Stand close to younger children as they move towards the giant, keeping the distance between the giant and the children fairly short. Let older children follow different instructions each time they play, for example, walk on tiptoe or hop.

### Home links

● Provide simple goose-shaped outlines for the children to take home and decorate using gold paint, feathers and glitter.

### Further ideas

● Use a musical instrument, such as bells or a tambourine, instead of the goose to make the game more challenging.

**Sarah Dix** is an assistant nursery teacher.

# Grow your own

**Build up an appetite with a fun game before enjoying the fruits of your labours at snack time!**

## Red tomatoes

**Stepping Stones:** show curiosity, observe and manipulate objects; describe simple features of objects and events; examine objects and living things to find out more about them (KUW).

**Early Learning Goals:** investigate objects and materials by using all of their senses as appropriate; find out about, and identify, some features of living things, objects and events they observe (KUW).

**Group size:** whole group.

### What you need

Growbags or planting pots; young tomato plants; seed and plant catalogues; bread; butter; cheese.

### What to do

● Check for any food allergies or dietary requirements.

● Look at the seed and plant catalogues. Explain that you are going to grow your own tomatoes.

● Discuss things that the plants will need in order to grow, such as sunlight, water and perhaps some special tomato food.

● Ask the children to help you prepare and plant the growbags or pots. Position them near a sunny wall or inside by a window.

● Over the next few weeks, watch the plants grow. Handle them gently, and supervise when the children are weeding and watering.

● When you have a few tomatoes, pick one or two green ones and put them on a window ledge to ripen.

● Make snack-time treats, such as cheese and tomato sandwiches.

### Support and extension

Buy mature tomato plants for younger children and enjoy picking the fruits together. Older children could keep a record of growth for their tomato plants.

### Home links

● Encourage parents to help their children find products that contain tomatoes at home. Ask them to bring them in to make a display.

© Gaynor Berry

## Fast food

**Stepping Stone:** negotiate space successfully when playing racing and chasing games with other children (PD).

**Early Learning Goal:** move with confidence, imagination and in safety (PD).

**Group size:** whole group.

### What you need

Four trikes or sit-on vehicles; circles of card in four different colours to represent different pizza toppings – yellow for cheese, red for pepperoni, white for chicken and brown for mushroom (you will need 16 pizzas in total, four of each colour); chalk in the same four colours.

### What to do

● Talk about take-away food with the children. Has anyone ever had any food delivered to their house? What did they order? Who delivered it?

● Draw a chalk mark on the floor in each of the four colours to represent four houses.

● Explain that you are going to play a game and the object is to deliver the pizzas to each house, one at a time. The red pizzas should be delivered to the red house and so on.

● Choose four volunteers to be the delivery people and invite the rest of the children to wait at the houses. Each delivery person must make four journeys, delivering one pizza to each of the houses. In between every delivery, they should return to the 'shop' to collect the pizza for the next house.

● Arrange the pizzas in four piles, so that each child delivers one pizza to each house.

● Repeat the activity two or three times until everyone has had a turn at being the delivery person.

### Support and extension

Direct younger children to the different houses. Challenge older children by introducing a time limit by which they have to deliver the pizzas to the correct houses.

### Further idea

● Collect together some foods that are made from or contain tomatoes, such as ketchup, tomato purée, pasta sauce and sun-dried tomatoes. Enjoy tasting them and using them in different recipes.

**Val Jeans-Jakobsson** is a teacher and writer.

# Tall, tall trees

**Find out all about trees with these fun and easy outdoor activities**

## Five little leaves
**Stepping Stone:** move body position as necessary (PD).
**Early Learning Goal:** show awareness of space, of themselves and of others (PD).
**Group size:** six to eight children.

### What you need
Two 1m lengths of ribbon; chalk.

### What to do
● Mark the outline of a large tree on the ground with chalk.
● Stand on the tree with the children and sing this traditional rhyme from *This Little Puffin...* compiled by Elizabeth Matterson (Puffin Books):

> *Five little leaves so bright and gay,*
> *Were dancing around on the tree one day.*
> *The wind came blowing through the town*
> *Whooooooooo... Whooooooooo*
> *And one little leaf came tumbling down.*

● Give a ribbon to two children and ask them to pretend to be the wind.
● As you sing the song again, encourage the 'wind' children to run around the tree, in and out of the other children. The other children must not move their feet, but may duck and bend to move out of the way of the 'wind' (ribbons).
● When the ribbons touch the children, they should sit down. How many children are left at the end of the song?

● Invite the children to take turns to be the wind while the rest of the group sing the song.

### Support and extension
Let younger children feel the wind by running around outdoors with their ribbons. Encourage older children to think of other ways that they can pretend to be the wind.

© Louise Gardner

### Home links
● Ask parents to bring a wooden object from home. Display them alongside some wooden logs, branches, wood shavings and leaves.

● Put a log slice in the entrance area. Encourage parents and children to count the rings together and guess how old the tree *was*.

## Tree treasure
**Stepping Stone:** show curiosity, observe and manipulate objects (KUW).
**Early Learning Goal:** investigate objects and materials by using all of their senses as appropriate (KUW).
**Group size:** four children.

### What you need
Twigs; branches; sticks; bark; raffia or string; leaves; card; paper; fir cones; corks; magnifying glasses; newspapers; safety scissors.

### What to do
● Spread out all of the natural resources on the ground and encourage the children to look at them carefully.
● Talk about the different features of the items, for example, how they feel, smell, look, what they are made of, where they have come from and what they might be used for.
● Let the children explore the different materials and help them to build different things, for example, prod the twigs and sticks through the paper, fasten the sticks together with the string and thread leaves on to the twigs.
● As you play alongside the children, comment on what they are doing and investigate the different materials together.

### Support and extension
Help younger children to stack the materials up to build simple towers or create tiny dens for play people. Encourage older children to name the different parts of the tree and describe the size, weight and position of the various resources.

### Further ideas
● Thread leaves on to lengths of raffia to create natural mobiles.

● Build tiny nests with leaves and moss into the crooks of fallen branches

**Clare Beswick** is an early years and childcare consultant.

# Shady structures

**Enjoy the sunshine as you explore the changing shadows throughout the day**

## Shadows from the sun

**Stepping Stone:** use size language such as 'big' and 'little' (MD).
**Early Learning Goal:** use language such as 'circle' or 'bigger' to describe the shape and size of solids and flat shapes (MD).
**Group size:** four to six children.

### What you need
Large, empty outdoor area with a hard surface; sunny day; large wooden or plastic bricks; chalk.

### What to do
● Invite the children to build large structures using the bricks on a sunny flat area.
● As the children work, encourage them to talk about the different shapes and sizes of the bricks.
● Once the models are finished, help the children to draw around the shadows cast by each of the structures with chalk.
● Leave the structures standing, then towards the end of the session, take the children back to them.
● Encourage the children to look at the shadows of the blocks. Are the shadows the same shape and size as the outlines that they drew earlier?
● Explain to the children that the sun rises at the beginning of the day, and during the morning, shadows shorten, until at midday they are at

© Eyewire

their shortest. Then during the afternoon, the sun starts to fall again and the shadows lengthen before disappearing at night.

### Support and extension
Help younger children to draw around their structure's shadow on white paper and cut the shadows out. Compare the shadows at the end of the session with the paper cut-outs. Encourage older children to predict the size of their shadows at the end of the session, and help them to draw a proposed chalk outline.

## Sundial shadows
**Stepping Stone:** initiate conversation, attend to and take account of what others say, and use talk to resolve disagreements (CLL).
**Early Learning Goal:** interact with others, negotiating plans and activities and taking turns in conversation (CLL).
**Group size:** four to six children.

### What you need
Large outdoor area; sunny day; felt-tipped pens. For each child: large white card circle; lump of modelling clay; pencil.

### Preparation
Make a sundial for each child by placing a flattened lump of modelling clay in the centre of a large, white card circle. Turn the card over and push a pencil into the centre of the circle until it is wedged into the clay.

### What to do
● Explain to the children that sundials were used to tell the time before wrist watches and clocks. Numbers were written around the edge

of the sundial to show hours and there was a spike in the middle of the dial. People 'read' the time by looking at where the shadow fell, which was cast by a spike in the middle of the dial.
● Invite the children to find a sunny place on the floor to put their sundials.
● Look together at the shadow that has been made by the pencil on one of the sundials. Invite the children to say why there is a shadow.
● Help each child to draw along the shadow on their sundial with a felt-tipped pen.
● Leave the sundials for an hour, then invite the children to find the shadow on their sundial and to draw on top of it again.
● Encourage the children to take turns to talk about what has happened to the shadow and why. Explain that the sun is constantly moving throughout the day, so the shadows also move.

### Support and extension
Help younger children to take turns and ask them to listen to the others while they are talking. Invite older children to describe how they could make more permanent sundials using plastics and wood.

## Home links
● Encourage parents to look for clocks and places where we need to read the time, for example, bus and train stations, cinema foyers and so on, when they are out with their children.

## Further idea
● Make pendulum pictures. Tie some string to the top of a cardboard cone. Fill the cone with sand. Then cut the pointed end off the cone. Put your finger over the hole until the cone is over the floor or a sheet of paper. Remove your finger and swing the pendulum from side to side to leave a trail of sand.

**Lorraine Gale** is a teacher and writer.

# Chapter 2
# Cookery

You'll find the perfect ingredients for some exciting cookery sessions in this chapter. Ensure that everyone gets involved by letting the children help to prepare the ingredients and tidy away afterwards before enjoying the fruits of their labours!

# Gingerbread fun

**Focus on parts of the body and have fun making gingerbread men with this simple recipe**

**Stepping Stone:** explore malleable materials by patting, stroking, poking, squeezing, pinching and twisting them (PD).

**Early Learning Goal:** handle tools, objects, construction and malleable materials safely and with increasing control (PD).

**Group size:** four children.

## What you need

**Ingredients:** 110g self raising flour; 50g margarine; 40g granulated sugar; 1 heaped tsp ground ginger; 1 level tsp bicarbonate of soda; 2 heaped tbsp golden syrup. (This makes around 12 small gingerbread men.)

**Equipment:** An oven pre-heated to 190ºc; gingerbread man cutters; weighing scales; four small mixing bowls; four wooden spoons; baking trays; greaseproof paper; aprons; sieve; hot water; tablespoon; copy of *The Gingerbread Man* (Ladybird Favourite Tales).

## Preparation

Check for food allergies and dietary requirements.

## What to do

● Read the story of *The Gingerbread Man*, encouraging the children to join in as much as possible with the refrain 'Run, run as fast as you can, you can't catch me, I'm the Gingerbread Man!'.

● Ask the children to identify the body parts of the gingerbread man, such as the head, mouth, nose, eyes, arms and legs.

● Compare the similarities and differences between the gingerbread man's body and theirs. Which parts are missing? Can you see his ears/fingers/toes? Invite the children to help make some gingerbread men.

● Invite the whole group to watch as you weigh out the ingredients, then divide the ingredients into four bowls and choose four children to cook first.

● Read out the ingredients using standard measure language but back this up with non-standard measures such as '40g of sugar, that's about a cup full' so that the children can compare visually and have a more concrete idea of weight in their minds as you are doing this.

© Soda

© PhotoDisc

● Begin by inviting the children to sift the flour, ginger and bicarbonate of soda into their bowls. Demonstrate how to lightly rub in the margarine with their fingers until the mixture is crumbly.

● Next add the syrup and encourage the children to mix until they have formed a thick paste. (Dipping the spoon into hot water first, and in between spoonfuls, will help the syrup to slide easily from the spoon.)

● Invite the children to divide their mixture into four balls of even size, flatten each with their palm and then use the cutter to make four gingerbread men.

● Write the children's names in pencil on the greaseproof paper section where they have placed their gingerbread men, then put into the oven for ten to 15 minutes.

## Support and extension

Less confident children will benefit from more practical guidance in the cookery activity, while the more able can be encouraged to work as independently as possible. Early finishers could enjoy paired reading of the story or draw a story map of the main events and key characters.

### Further ideas

● Using play dough, Plasticine or leftover mixture from the recipe, let the children make models of their own bodies, trying to remember as many body parts as possible!

● Visit a real bakery to see lots of gingerbread men being made all at once, or take a trip to a local bakery to buy some as a treat.

### Home links

● Do not be afraid to get messy! Invite a carer to come in and help with the cooking.

**Martine Horvath** is a Reception teacher.

# White Christmas

Make a delicious alternative treat for Father Christmas as he delivers presents in sunny weather!

**Stepping Stone:** gain an awareness of the cultures and beliefs of others (KUW).
**Early Learning Goal:** begin to know about their own cultures and beliefs and those of other people.
**Group size:** four children (KUW).
**Preparation time:** 15 minutes.
**Cooking time:** five minutes.

## What you need
**Ingredients:** 3 cups of rice crispies; 1 cup of desiccated coconut; half a cup of powdered milk; half a cup of icing sugar; quarter cup of red and/or green glacé cherries chopped; quarter cup of raisins/sultanas; 300g white chocolate (chopped). This makes about 20 pieces of cake.
**Equipment:** cooking facilities; boiling water; large sharp knife (all adult use only); atlas or globe; large pan; large heat-proof bowl; weighing scales; four small mixing bowls; four small square tins lined with greaseproof paper; four wooden spoons; aprons; food bags.

## Preparation
Check for food allergies and dietary requirements.

## What to do
● Show the children Australia in an atlas or on a globe and explain that it is summer there when it is winter in England.
● Explain that when Father Christmas delivers presents in England he likes to eat spicy, warm mince pies, but because it is so hot in Australia, he prefers something cold! Invite the children to help you make some White Christmas Cake – an Australian cold sweet.
● Let the children take turns in measuring out the correct ingredients. Place them in the middle of a table so that everyone can see clearly.
● An adult should divide all the dry ingredients (except the white chocolate) into four bowls.

© Louise Gardner

© Louise Gardner

● Let the children mix the rice crispies, coconut, powdered milk, icing sugar and fruit with a wooden spoon, ready for the melted chocolate to be poured on top.
● At a safe distance, heat some water slowly in a large pan and place the heat-proof bowl over the pan. Talk about the dangers of boiling water so that the children understand why an adult must do this part of the recipe.
● Add the chopped white chocolate to the bowl and let the children watch the melting process. Ask questions such as 'What makes the chocolate melt?' and 'How could we make it hard again?'.
● Evenly divide the dry ingredients and melted chocolate into the children's bowls and encourage them to mix it in thoroughly.
● Give each child a small lined tin and invite them to press their mixture into it. Place the tins in the fridge until set.
● Remove from the fridge and leave to stand for five minutes then, highlighting safety aspects, cut into pieces. Ask the children to help you share them out evenly.

## Support and extension
Guide younger children with plenty of practical help. Allow older children to be as independent as possible.

## Further ideas
● Write a letter to Father Christmas asking him what it is like in Australia.

● Draw a picture of Father Christmas wearing appropriate clothing as he delivers presents in a hot climate.

## Home links
● If you have any carers who have lived in a hot climate, invite them to talk about the kinds of food or recipes they may have for Father Christmas.

**Martine Horvath** is a Reception teacher.

# Cookery
# Winter warmers

**Promote healthy eating by making and tasting traditional recipes for some comforting winter treats**

## Pasties and puds!

**Stepping Stone:** show awareness of a range of healthy practices with regard to eating and hygiene (PD).

**Early Learning Goal:** recognise the importance of keeping healthy and those things which contribute to this (PD).

**Group size:** four children.

### What you need

**Ingredients for four pasties:**
250g plain flour; 125g margarine; water; extra flour to roll out pastry; 1 small diced potato; 1 diced onion; 75g grated mild cheese; 1 beaten egg; pinch of salt.

**Equipment:** bowl; tablespoon; blunt knives; fork; pastry brush; baking tray; saucer; rolling pin; measuring scales; aprons.

### Preparation

Check for food allergies and dietary requirements.

### What to do

● Ask the children to brainstorm all of their favourite hot foods to eat in winter. Discuss why it is important to eat a healthy and balanced diet.

● Make the pastry with the children asking them to watch carefully to see how the ingredients change. Invite them to help you mix the flour, salt and margarine together with their fingertips until it looks like breadcrumbs. Add a little water until you have made a damp ball.

● Divide the mixture evenly, then help the children to roll their pastry out on to a floured surface to a thickness of about half a centimetre. Dust the rolling pins with flour to prevent sticking.

● Roll out until the pastry is large enough to place a saucer on top. Support the children as they cut around the saucer with a blunt knife.

● Place the pastry circles on to a greased tray. Invite the children to put a tablespoon of potato, onion and cheese in the middle of their pastry.

● Fold over the pastry and demonstrate how to press the edges firmly together to seal them. Finish by pressing a fork around the edges. Prick the pasties with a fork.

● Ask the children to use a pastry brush to paint egg over their pasties, explaining that this will help to brown them. Bake the pasties for 30 to 35 minutes at 180°C, 350°F, Gas Mark 4.

© Louise Gardner

### What you need

**Ingredients for rice pudding:** margarine; 40g rice; 25g caster sugar; 1 teaspoon of ground nutmeg or mixed spice (optional); 625ml milk.

**Equipment:** ovenproof dish; sieve; measuring jug; tablespoon; aprons; weighing scales.

### What to do

● Smear the dish with margarine. Wash the rice well and place into the dish with the nutmeg and/or mixed spice.

● Pour on the milk and let each child place a knob of margarine or butter on top then bake in the oven for 30 minutes at 150°C, 300°F, Gas Mark 2.

● After 30 minutes, remove the mixture from the oven, explaining to the children the safety precaution of using oven gloves. Give the mixture a good stir, then put it back in the oven.

● Leave the pudding to cook for an hour and a half until creamy with a brown skin. Enjoy sharing your pasties and puddings on a cold winter's day.

### Further ideas

● Make a warm drink such as hot chocolate together.

● Make a 'favourite winter warmer foods' concertina booklet with each child.

### Home links

● Invite carers to help prepare vegetable soup or a winter warmer recipe of their choice.

**Martine Horvath** is a Reception teacher.

# Delicious dinosaurs!

**Encourage everybody to join in with this recipe idea to make some tasty prehistoric treats**

**Stepping Stone:** engage in activities requiring hand-eye coordination (PD).
**Early Learning Goal:** to handle tools and malleable materials safely and with increasing control (PD).
**Group size:** up to six children.

## What you need

**Ingredients:** 25g margarine; 50g plain flour; ⅛ tsp baking powder; ½ tbsp brown sugar; 1 tbsp golden syrup; ½ tsp ground ginger; currants. (This amount is per child and will make about three dinosaurs.)
**Equipment:** oven; blunt knife; mixing bowls; sieve; tablespoon; teaspoon; wooden spoons; greased baking tray; rolling-pins; dinosaur shape cutters (or home-made templates); cooling tray; fish slice.

## Preparation

Check for food allergies and dietary requirements. Pre-heat the oven to 180°C, Gas Mark 4.

© Louise Gardner

## What to do

● Ensure that all surfaces are clean and hygienic and that you have all washed your hands thoroughly.
● Recap on some of the dinosaur names and shapes that you have been finding out about, then invite the children to make some dinosaur biscuits.
● Give each child a bowl containing margarine. Help the children to cut the margarine into small pieces using a blunt knife.
● Let each child take a turn to sift the flour and baking powder on to their margarine encouraging the others to wait patiently and watch what is going on.
● Show the children how to rub the fat into the flour until it looks like breadcrumbs.

© Louise Gardner

● Let each child in turn spoon the correct amount of sugar, ginger and syrup into their bowl and then invite them to stir the mixture carefully using a wooden spoon. Provide help with the mixing stage when necessary.
● Once the ingredients are well mixed, invite the children to knead their mixture into a lump with their hands, adding more flour if it gets too sticky.
● Finally, demonstrate how to coat the rolling-pin in flour and then, on a floured surface, help the children to roll out the dough to less than 1cm thickness.
● Let the children use the dinosaur templates to cut out their shapes and add a currant eye.
● Invite them to gather leftover pieces into a ball and roll out again to make more dinosaurs.
● Using the fish slice, carefully lift the biscuits and place them well spread out on to the tray to bake for 15–20 minutes until they are a rich brown colour.
● Leave the biscuits on a wire tray to cool while the children tidy their working area and wash and dry the equipment.

## Support and extension

Work with only two or three very young children so that you can give them the practical help as necessary. Encourage older children to measure out their own ingredients and do as much as possible for themselves, sharing the equipment and working together whenever necessary.

## Further ideas

● Practise manipulative skills by cutting around the dinosaur templates on to play dough.

● Mix up some papier maché and invite the children to make 3-D models of their favourite dinosaur.

## Home links

● Let the children eat one biscuit and take the remainder home to share with their families.

**Barbara J Leach** was previously head of a 4+ Unit in Leicestershire.

# Cookery
# Bunnies in burrows

**Try this simple cookery idea to make some underground animal treats**

© Louise Gardner

**Stepping Stone:** show curiosity and observation by talking about shapes; adapt shapes (MD).
**Early Learning Goal:** use language such as 'circle' or 'bigger' to describe the shape and size of solids and flat shapes (MD).
**Group size:** four children.

## What you need
**Ingredients:** muffins (halved) or crumpets; cheese slices; pitted olives; carrots; tinned sweetcorn; peas.
**Equipment:** grill (adult use); sharp knife (adult use); circular pastry cutters (or cups and blunt knives); bowls; pictures, posters and books about underground animals.

## Preparation
Cut some of the carrots into small sticks to make the rabbits' whiskers, and into thin triangles for the ears. Check for food allergies and dietary requirements. Make an example rabbit muffin to show to the children. Put each of the ingredients into individual bowls.

## What to do
● Ensure that all surfaces are clean, then roll up sleeves, wash hands and put on aprons.
● Begin by talking about animals that live underground. Show the children the pictures, posters and books, and talk about the underground burrows and holes that rabbits and moles live in.
● Show the children your prepared rabbit muffin and talk about the different ingredients that you used to make it. What shapes can they see? What shape is the muffin? The cheese slices? What shape are the rabbit's ears? Invite the children to have a go at making their own rabbit muffins.
● Let the children select a muffin or crumpet to decorate, and show them the bowls of individual ingredients.

● Begin by adding a layer of cheese to each muffin. Look at the shape of the cheese slice. Will this fit on to the muffin? Why not? Ask the children for suggestions of ways that you could make the cheese fit.
● Let the children use the pastry cutters to cut out a cheese circle, or place cups on top of the cheese slices and cut around them using blunt knives.
● Talk about the next thing that you will need to add. Give the children plenty of time to select the ingredients that they need to decorate their rabbits. Provide help and suggestions as necessary. Encourage the children to tuck the rabbits' carrot ears underneath the cheese slices so that they do not fall off when they are cooking!

© Louise Gardner

● When everyone is happy with their rabbits, carefully move them on to a grill pan and place under the grill for a few minutes until the cheese bubbles.
● Leave the rabbits to cool, then invite the children to have a look at them. What has changed? Does the cheese look the same as when they put it on?
● Enjoy eating your rabbits at snack time.

## Further ideas
● Provide paper plates and coloured paper shapes. Invite the children to recreate their rabbit faces on the plates, then display them on the wall.

● Try making other faces on the muffins, such as owls. Can the children make their own faces?

## Home links
● With parental consent, take pictures of the children making their muffins. Compile these into a book and invite the children to share it with their carers.

# Snake bites!

**Enjoy some hands-on cookery fun with this simple recipe to make delicious slithery snakes!**

**Stepping Stone:** begin to describe the texture of things (CD).

**Early Learning Goal:** explore colour, texture, shape and form in three dimensions.

**Group size:** four children.

## What you need

**Ingredients for four snakes:** one heaped tablespoon of margarine or butter; approximately 20 marshmallows or two cupfuls of miniature marshmallows; three cupfuls of puffed rice cereal.

**To decorate:** jelly sweets and liquorice bootlaces in different colours (cut the bootlaces into different lengths and place in individual bowls).

**Equipment:** microwave; microwave-safe mixing bowl; greased trays; metal spoons.

## Preparation

Check for food allergies and dietary requirements.

## What to do

● Ensure that surfaces are clean, then roll up sleeves, wash hands and put on aprons.

● Begin by talking about some of the jungle animals that the children know about. Talk about snakes and invite the children to offer descriptive words to suggest what snakes look like, and how they might feel and sound, such as slippery, stripy, wiggly, hissing and so on.

● Explain to the children that you are going to have fun making some slithery snakes.

● Investigate the different ingredients, noticing the texture, shapes and smells. Put the margarine or butter and marshmallows into the bowl and melt in the microwave on 'High' for one minute.

● Carefully remove the bowl, then on a safe surface, invite each child to take a turn at stirring the mixture. What has happened?

● Put the bowl back into the microwave and cook on 'High' for another minute, then stir again.

● Next, tip in the cups of puffed rice. Again, let the children take turns to stir until the rice is thoroughly coated with the melted marshmallows.

● While the mixture is cooling for a couple of minutes, place a sliver of butter on each child's hands and invite them to rub their hands together to melt the butter. This will prevent the mixture from sticking to their hands.

● Invite each child to take a generous portion of the mixture and place it on to a greased tray before moulding it into their desired shape of snake. As they mould the mixture, encourage them to describe what it feels like, introducing words such as slimy, knobbly, bumpy and so on.

● When the children are happy with their snakes, ask them to wash their hands before returning to decorate them. Let the children enjoy choosing colours and shapes to make their snakes as weird and wonderful as they wish!

● Place the snakes in a cool place and then have fun describing and comparing them before you enjoy them at snack time.

## Further ideas

● Make a list of words that the children use throughout the activity such as melt, mix, squishy, gooey and so on. Display these around photographs of the children's finished snakes.

● Rather than shaping the mixture while warm, press it into a greased baking tray. When set, press out shapes using animal cutters, then have fun decorating them.

## Home links

● This recipe is ideal for making and adapting at home. Invite carers to try it with their children using smaller quantities of ingredients, and to make different animals.

© Louise Gardner

## Cookery

# What's cooking?

**Investigate changes that happen when food is heated and cooled with this tasty recipe for fudge**

**Stepping Stone:** show an awareness of change (KUW).
**Early Learning Goal:** look closely at similarities, differences, patterns and change (KUW).
**Group size:** *small groups.*

## What you need

Two small packets of milk chocolate buttons; 397g tin of condensed milk; 2oz butter or margarine; plastic mixing bowl; microwave; tin opener; fridge; greased dish (20cm by 20cm); 'hundreds and thousands' decorations; mixing spoon; aprons.

© Louise Gardner

## What to do

● Check for food allergies and dietary requirements.
● Ask the children to wash their hands and put on aprons.
● Invite the children to pour the condensed milk into the mixing bowl, then add the margarine.
● Encourage them to observe the liquid form of the milk and solid form of the margarine.
● Draw the children's attention to the solid shape of the chocolate buttons, before asking them to place them in the bowl.
● Put the bowl in the microwave and heat on a medium temperature for approximately ten minutes. Let the children stir regularly throughout the cooking process. Notice how the margarine and chocolate melt, changing the colour of the milk and margarine.

● Explain that heat has caused the buttons to melt, changing their form to a liquid.
● Look at the mixture through the microwave's glass door. When it starts to thicken and rise in the bowl remove with caution as it will be very hot!
● Let the children stir in the 'hundreds and thousands'. Notice that as the mixture is still hot, but already beginning to cool, some will melt and their colours run whereas others will not.
● Pour the mixture into the greased dish and place in the fridge to set. Once set, remove the dish from the fridge and encourage the children to talk about the changes that the mixture has undergone from the time it was placed in the fridge to its now solid form.
● Cut the fudge into squares and share equally between the children.

## Support and extension

Work with no more than two to three younger children at a time. Ask older children to think of additional extras to add to the fudge instead of 'hundreds and thousands', such as cut-up cherries. Would these change when they are heated?

© Louise Gardner

## Further ideas

● Change the fudge recipe by adding food colouring in place of the chocolate buttons. You could try adding pink food colouring and strawberry essence or green colouring with peppermint essence.

● For some dramatic changes, enjoy the excitement of making microwave popcorn!

## Home links

● Send home a copy of the fudge recipe for the children to share with their parents and carers.

**Lisa Bessinger** is a former nursery school principal who works as a company director and writer.

# Sweet sheep

**Enjoy this simple cookery idea to make fluffy meringue sheep**

**Stepping Stone:** use simple tools to effect changes to materials (PD).
**Early Learning Goal:** handle tools and malleable materials safely and with increasing control;
**Group size:** four children at a time.

## What you need
**Ingredients:** two egg whites, vanilla essence; ¼ tsp of cream of tartar; 4oz (110g) caster sugar; chocolate drops; chocolate fingers or flakes.
**Equipment:** oven; two large baking trays; brown paper or foil; decorating bag fitted with a 1cm round tip.

## Preparation
Pre-heat the oven to 300°F/150°C/Gas Mark 2. Check for food allergies and dietary requirements.

## What to do
● Ensure that all work surfaces are clean and that all the children have washed their hands.
● Begin by talking about different animals that appear in nursery rhymes. Tell the children that they are going to have some fun making their own tasty meringue sheep.
● Invite the children to line two large baking trays with brown paper or foil.
● Give each child a small bowl and help them to beat the egg white, two drops of vanilla essence and cream of tartar together until soft peaks form.
● Gradually let each child, in turn, add the sugar to their mixture, beating it until stiff peaks are formed.
● Once the ingredients are well mixed, invite the children to half fill a decorating bag with the egg white mixture.

● Let the children gently squeeze the bag to form a 5cm diameter circle on the baking tray. Make another slightly smaller circle for the head of the sheep.
● Once all the ingredients have been used, invite the children to place one chocolate drop on each sheep for the eyes.
● Bake in the oven for ten to 12 minutes or until the meringues just start to turn golden.
● Turn the oven off and leave the meringues to dry in the oven with the door closed for approximately 30 minutes. Invite the children to help tidy the area and wash and dry the equipment.
● Remove from the oven and leave until cool enough to decorate. Invite the children to use chocolate fingers or flakes to make legs for the sheep. Put on a plate ready to share.

## Support and extension
Work with just two or three younger children at a time so that you can offer practical help as necessary. Encourage older children to measure out their own ingredients. Challenge them to make animals from other nursery rhymes.

## Further ideas
● Make sheep and other animals with play dough or Plasticine. Take photographs of each stage to make a step-by step recipe card for future use.

● Talk about the change from the liquid egg white into the solid meringue, and the colour change from clear to white once the egg white has been whisked.

## Home links
● Let the children eat one meringue and take the remainder home to share with their families.

● Provide a copy of the recipe for carers to try at home with their children.

**Sharon Campbell** is a senior nursery nurse and freelance writer.

## Cookery
# Fancy fish cakes
**Enjoy this simple cookery idea to make some healthy snack-time treats**

**Stepping Stone:** begin to try out a range of tools and techniques safely (KUW).
**Early Learning Goal:** select the tools and techniques they need to shape, assemble and join materials they are using (KUW).
**Group size:** four children at a time.

## What you need
Books or pictures showing fishermen and fishing trawlers.
**Ingredients:**
200g tuna, drained and flaked; 450g potatoes, peeled and boiled; 25g butter or margarine; tbsp milk (optional); tbsp chopped fresh parsley; pepper; finely grated rind of half a lemon; tbsp plain flour; tbsp cooking oil.
**Equipment:** large mixing bowl; four small bowls; mixing spoons; forks; grater; rolling-pin; round cutter; grill; grill pan.

## Preparation
Check for food allergies and dietary requirements.

## What to do
● Ensure that all work surfaces are clean and that the children have washed their hands and put on aprons.
● Begin by talking about different types of fish. Explain that the fish that we see in the supermarket have been caught in the sea. What do we call people who catch fish? If possible, show the children pictures of fishermen and trawlers with their hauls of fish.
● Tell the children that they are going to have some fun making their own tasty fish cakes.
● Show the children the ingredients. Divide the tuna equally between four bowls and give one bowl to each child. Encourage the children to mash their tuna using a fork.
● In a large bowl, mash the potatoes with the butter or margarine, adding milk if the mixture seems a little too dry.
● Let each child gradually add the tuna, parsley, pepper to taste and lemon rind to the large bowl.

Mix the ingredients together well.
● Once the ingredients are thoroughly mixed, invite the children to lightly flour their hands, and to take a handful of the mixture. Show them how to shape it into round cakes, approximately 2cm thick.
● Next, let the children watch you brush the grill pan with oil and arrange the cakes on it.
● Dab the fish cakes with a little more oil.
● Reinforce the safety issues of using a cooker and grill, then cook the fishcakes under a pre-heated moderate grill for four to five minutes on each side, until golden brown.
● Leave to cool on a plate, ready to be shared at snack time!
● Ask the children to help tidy the area and wash and dry the equipment.

## Support and extension
Work with just two or three younger children at a time so that you can offer practical help as necessary. Encourage older children to measure out their own ingredients. Challenge them to make a fish-shaped fresh salad from lettuce, carrots, sweetcorn and sliced tomatoes.

## Further ideas
● Make fish with play dough or salt dough. Take photographs of each stage to make a step-by-step recipe card for future use.

● Design and make a fish from papier-mâché materials, using a variety of craft materials to decorate it.

## Home links
● Provide a copy of the recipe for parents to try at home with their children.

**Sharon Campbell**
is a senior nursery nurse and freelance writer.

# Our daily bread

**Make a healthy snack-time treat with this simple cookery idea**

**Stepping Stone:** show an awareness of change (KUW).
**Early Learning Goal:** look closely at similarities, differences, patterns and change (KUW).
**Group size:** eight children.

## What you need
**Ingredients:** 200g plain flour; 25g solid vegetable fat; 12g fresh yeast; 1 tsp lemon juice; 125ml warmed milk or water; ½ tsp salt; ½ tsp castor sugar.
**Equipment:** aprons; scales; teaspoon; measuring jug; sieve; baking tray; mixing bowls; small bowl (for the yeast); plastic bag; microwave oven; conventional oven.
**General:** different breads such as wholemeal, white, pitta, chapatti, rye and baguette.

## Preparation
Check for any food allergies and dietary requirements.

## What to do
● Bread-making is an ideal cookery activity for young children. The dough will not spoil with over handling so they can become fully involved. Help to speed up the proving process by adding lemon juice to the yeast, ensuring that even those children who are with you for just part of the day can join in.
● Ask the children if they can think of any foods that are grown in the countryside, such as vegetables and fruit. Explain that one of our favourite foods, bread, is made from wheat, which is grown in big fields. Show the children the different types of bread and invite them to describe, smell and, if they wish, taste a few of them.

● Explain that you are going to make your own bread to enjoy at snack time.
● At each stage, discuss the changes that take place. Encourage the children to use their senses: looking, smelling, feeling, tasting and even listening.
● Put on aprons, wash hands and tie hair back.
● Invite the children to help you sieve the flour into the bowl. Rub in the fat and salt until it resembles fine breadcrumbs. Cream the yeast and sugar together in a small bowl.
● When this turns to liquid, add the lemon juice. Next, stir in a little warmed milk or water to the yeast.
● Add this to the flour mixture, together with enough of the remaining liquid to make a soft, but not sticky, dough. Place the dough in a microwave and prove for 30 seconds on full power. Remove and knead thoroughly on a floured surface.
● Divide the dough into pieces so that each child can shape it into a round ball. Put on a greased baking tray in a warm place or wrapped in a plastic bag for two or three minutes.
● Bake in a hot oven (230°C/450°F/Gas Mark 8) for eight to ten minutes until well risen and golden brown.
● Allow the bread to cool before enjoying it together at snack time.

## Support and extension
Help younger children with the sieving, mixing and kneading. Let older children form the dough into animal shapes, such as a hedgehog, pinching out spines and making indented eyes and a nose.

### Further ideas
● Compare fresh and dried yeast. Talk about the texture and smell.

● Grind pieces of wheat (available at florists) to discover how flour is made.

● Read the story **The Little Red Hen** (First Favourite Tales series, Ladybird Books).

### Home links
● Share the recipe with parents.

● Invite children from different backgrounds to discuss the kinds of bread that they eat at home.

**Lorraine Frankish** is an early years tutor and NVQ Assessor.

© Louise Gardner

# Cookery

# A snack a day

**Plan a week of snack-time treats as you introduce the children to the different food groups with these activities**

© Ingram publishing

© Digital Vision Ltd.

© Image Source Ltd.

© Andrea Lewis

© Andrea Lewis

**Stepping Stone:** show awareness of a range of healthy practices with regard to eating, sleeping and hygiene (PD).

**Early Learning Goal:** recognise the importance of keeping healthy and those things which contribute to this (PD).

**Group size:** whole group for discussion; four children when preparing snacks.

## What you need

Utensils and ingredients to make the different snacks listed (see right).

## What to do

● Talk to the children about healthy foods. Explain that to keep their bodies healthy, give them energy and help them to grow, they need to eat a variety of foods from each food group. To stay healthy, we should eat more foods from the top two groups, and fewer from the bottom group, such as:
● bread, cereals and potatoes
● fruit and vegetables
● meat and fish
● milk and dairy foods
● fatty and sugary foods.
● Introduce the term 'five a day' to the children and explain that this means eating five pieces of fruit or vegetables each day as part of a healthy diet.
● Each day, for one week, introduce one of the food groups at snack time. Involve the children in preparing the snacks.

## Monday (bread):
### Little Red Hen's toast
● Add a few drops of food colouring to a bowl of milk. With a small, clean brush, let each child take turns to draw their initial on a slice of white bread using the coloured milk. Toast the bread in a toaster and see what happens.

## Tuesday (fruit and vegetables):
### Vegetable fun
● Cut assorted vegetables into shapes, such as carrot curls, radish fans, mushroom slices, celery branches, broccoli trees and cucumber circles. Let the children make pictures with the vegetable shapes on their plates before eating. Provide a dip to dunk the vegetables into.

## Wednesday (meat and fish):
### Animal antics
● Give each child three slices of wholemeal bread. Provide animal cutters and invite the children to cut out three identical shapes. Let the children choose fillings such as tuna mayonnaise, peanut butter and meat paste, and spread them on to two of their cut-outs. Top with the matching cut-out, then try to stand your animals up before eating them!

## Thursday (dairy):
### Butter fingers
● Place a pint of whipping cream and a teaspoon of salt into a small jar, and seal the lid tightly. Sit together in a circle and pass the jar around, inviting each child to shake the jar (place a clean marble in the jar to speed up the process). When the cream is thick and yellow, pour off any excess liquid and spread their 'butter' on to crackers to eat.

## Friday (sugar and fats):
### Sweet treats
● For a special treat, enjoy decorating ready-made fairy cakes with different-coloured icing. Encourage the children to pipe the initial letter of their name or position chocolate drops to make patterns on the cakes.

## Support and extension
Younger children can enjoy the daily healthy snacks without concentrating on the food groups. Encourage older children to keep a record of their 'five a day' eating.

## Home links
● Before beginning your food week, send a note to parents asking them to inform you of any food allergies or dietary requirements or food allergies that their child may have. Prepare alternatives for these children. Invite parents to assist in preparing snacks or share one of the tasting parties.

## Further ideas
● Cut out food pictures from magazines. Paste the pictures on to a large sheet of card to make a poster of the five food groups.

**Beverley Michael**
is an early years
writer.

# Chapter 3
# Displays

This chapter contains a selection of stunning displays that are guaranteed to bring a splash of colour to your walls. Help to make them truly interactive by adding interest tables to which the children can return again and again.

# All about us!

## Celebrate the way we look and the things that we can do with this colourful display

© Victoria Farrow

**Stepping Stone:** use simple tools and techniques competently and appropriately (KUW).
**Early Learning Goal:** select the tools and techniques they need to shape, assemble and join materials they are using (KUW).
**Group size:** whole group.

### What you need
Backing paper; powder paints; safety mirror; white card; paper fasteners; white sugar paper; paper plates; collage scraps; photograph of each child; children's names printed on to thin card.

### What to do
● Sit the children around you and show them the photographs and name cards. Identify each child together. Discuss the facial expressions, inviting the children to suggest what each child might be feeling. Read the name cards together and match them to the pictures.
● Point to and name the features on your face, then ask the children to do the same. Look at each other and then use the mirror.

● Invite the children to use their observations to make collage faces using paper plates painted in flesh tones and decorated with collage scraps.
● Ask about six children at a time to paint pictures of themselves on large pieces of sugar paper. When dry, cut out and attach to the board. Attach the photographs and name labels above, and the collage faces at the top.
● Make moving models to show different activities. Provide cut-out body parts that can be joined using paper fasteners. Encourage the children to colour in the shapes and assemble them to make complete bodies, then to choose an activity and adjust the limbs on their figure accordingly. Attach to the display using Blu-Tack and add labels.
● On the display table place some play people in family groups, puzzles, story and information books, and books that the children have made.
● Use the side of the display to measure the children and display their handprints.

### Using the display
#### Personal, social and emotional development
● Talk about how hands can be kind (helping to tidy up, look after a new baby or stroke a pet) or nasty (snatching or hitting).
● Discuss friendship. Look at how your display shows one big group of friends.

#### Communication, language and literacy
● Make books about 'Ourselves' with pictures of the children's families, homes, hand and footprints and so on.
● Introduce words to describe facial expressions.

#### Mathematical development
● Count pairs of eyes, numbers of legs, fingers and so on in the display.
● Make coloured card feet with shapes on, and place on the floor. Throw a dice and move the appropriate number of steps. What colour/shape have you landed on?

#### Knowledge and understanding of the world
● Use the play people figures to sort, count and name family members.
● Encourage the children to look positively at similarities and differences in each other.

#### Physical development
● During movement activities, think about how limbs move.

#### Creative development
● Make hand- and footprints in clay.

**Victoria Farrow** is a teacher and writer.

# Incy Wincy Spider

**Cheer up a rainy day with a colourful display based on this favourite rhyme**

**Stepping stone:** show care and concern for living things and the environment (PSED).
**Early Learning Goal:** understand what is right, what is wrong and why (PSED).
**Group size:** whole group.

## What you need

Dark backing paper; silver pen; paints; paintbrushes; balloon; papier mâché; two pulp balls; cardboard tubes; black sugar paper; sticky tape; silver card; cardboard egg-boxes; pipe-cleaners; 'googly' eyes.

## What to do

● Begin by taking about spiders. Discuss the webs that they make and how they use their webs to catch flies. Explain that even though we may not like them, we should never hurt spiders or destroy their webs.
● Cover the display board with dark paper and paint on a brick effect.
● Ask a small group of children to paint several cardboard tubes using grey paint. When dry, tape the tubes together to make Incy Wincy's drain pipe. An adult should attach the pipe to the wall with drawing pins or tape.
● Encourage another group to make spiders. Let each child paint a cardboard egg-box section black. When dry, an adult should make four small holes in each side. Show the children how to thread a pipe-cleaner through from one side to the other to make four pairs of legs. Stick on 'googly' eyes then attach to the display.
● Make a 3-D spider to sit at the top of the drainpipe. Help the children to cover a balloon with papier mâché. When dry, burst the balloon carefully with a pin. Paint the spider's body black and add two pulp ball eyes and strips of paper for legs.
● Make raindrops and puddles from

© Victoria Farrow

silver card. Suspend the raindrops above the display using thread. Add clouds cut from dark paper.
● To complete your display add a title and arrange wet weather resources, toys and books around the display.

### Using the display
### Personal, social and emotional development
● Discuss spiders and storms, then encourage the children to talk about things that frighten them. Conclude on a positive and reassuring note.

### Communication, language and literacy
● Enjoy learning the rhyme and actions for 'Incy Wincy Spider'.
● Go outside on a rainy day and listen to the sounds of the rain. Make up a sounds poem to add to your display.

### Mathematical development
● Dip the ends of cardboard cylinders in paint and print with them to make circles. Can the children suggest what shape they would see if they used the cylinder as a painting roller? Use sponge rollers to find out.

### Knowledge and understanding of the world
● On a wet day observe the water rushing out of the drainpipes. Find out how it gets there and where it goes to.
● Go outside on a misty day and look for spider webs around your setting.

### Physical development
● Put on wellies and have fun splashing in the puddles.

### Creative development
● Paint rainy day pictures by brushing the paper with water then painting on top and watching the colours run.
● Make storm music with percussion instruments, starting quietly and building up to a loud storm then dying away.

**Victoria Farrow** is a teacher and writer. **Fran Robinson** is a nursery nurse.

# All kinds of patterns

**Help to focus the children's attention by using just black and white to make this striking display**

### Stepping Stone:
Show an interest in shape and space by making arrangements with objects (MD).

### Early Learning Goal:
talk about, recognize and recreate simple patterns (MD).

**Group size:** small groups.

## What you need
Black and white backing paper; black and white sugar paper; black and white paint; black tissue paper; scissors; cotton-wool buds; patterned artefacts.

## Preparation
● This display works best if you use just black and white, as it helps to maintain the interest and focus on pattern, avoiding any attention being paid to colour.

● Make a collection of black and white spotted, striped, checked and zigzag artefacts. Gather together and talk about the different patterns. Reinforce the pattern names and encourage the children to contribute their understanding and awareness of pattern. Invite them to help you sort the objects into the four different categories.

● Challenge the children to find more black and white patterned artefacts at home to bring in and add to the collection.

## What to do
● Divide the display board into four areas. Label each part and attach the resources around the correct pattern names.

● Over four separate sessions, re-introduce each pattern and encourage small groups to help recreate the four types of pattern using different creative techniques.

© Sheila Dempsey

● Encourage the children to print spots with corks and cotton-wool buds using paint on sugar paper. Use scissors to cut squares of paper and build a chequerboard pattern. Tear and stick tissue stripes on to sugar paper and paint zigzags with brushes in a variety of thicknesses.

● When the work is complete, display it alongside the patterned artefacts.

● Add a title. Complete with a border, again using alternate black and white patterns.

**Sheila Dempsey** is a nursery teacher at Guthrie CE Infant and Nursery School, Calne, Wiltshire.

## Using the display
### Personal, social and emotional development
● Find out about different uniforms that have black and white patterns, such as a chef's trousers or a police officer's hat. Add pictures to your display.

### Communication, language and literacy
● Read stories featuring patterned characters such as zebras, Dalmatians and snakes.

● Make a story-book about the adventures of a favourite patterned toy in your setting. The children can be both illustrators and authors.

### Mathematical development
● Introduce simple chequerboard games such as 'Snakes and Ladders' or 'Ludo'.

● Use beads and pegboards to develop an understanding of repeating pattern.

### Knowledge and understanding of the world
● Find out about animals that use their patterned coats for camouflage. Add pictures or models to an interest table.

### Physical development
● Play pattern games outside. Divide a large area into four, each marked with a different chalk pattern. Tell the children that they must run to the correct area when you call out the pattern name.

### Creative development
● Have a spotty, stripy, check or zigzag day. Invite the children to come wearing appropriately-patterned clothes. Have plenty of spare accessories to hand!

# The paint machine

**Make a show of everything that you have found out about mixing and changing colours with this stunning display**

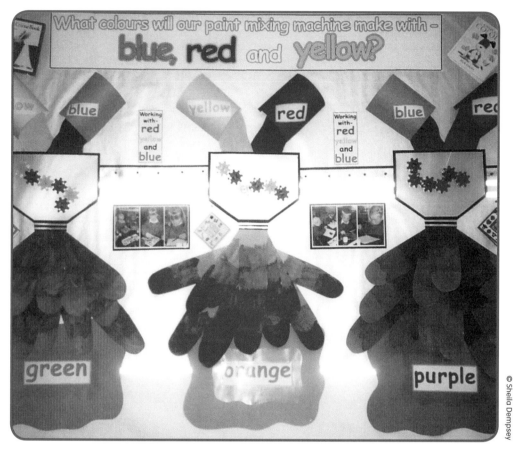

**Stepping Stone:** explore what happens when they mix colours (CD).
**Early Learning Goal:** explore colour, texture, shape, form and space in two or three dimensions (CD).
**Group size:** small groups.

## What you need

Silver backing paper; silver card; silver scraps; red, yellow and blue card; red, yellow and blue paint; strips of white sugar paper; black border paper; mixing palettes; red, yellow and blue construction cogs.

## What to do

● Over several sessions encourage the children to paint strips of sugar paper using three primary colours.
● Cover a display board with silver backing paper and use silver card to make a machine-like background, including three paint hoppers.
● At the top of the display, bend six different-coloured pieces of card to make six 'tins' of coloured paint.

● Frame the display with black border paper.
● Use some of the children's primary painting work to 'pour' from the appropriate-coloured tin into the machine hoppers. On the fronts of the hoppers, encourage the children to make coloured cog constructions using the appropriate colours.
● Discuss what will happen when the two colours mix in the machine.
● Fold strips of sugar paper into four sections, then ask the children to paint the first section with one colour. Give the children another colour and let them mix a little paint at a time into their original colour. As new colours are mixed the children can paint the next section of their paper strips.
● When the colour mix strips are complete add them to the display, to look as if they are splashing out of the machine.
● Add appropriate words to the finished display.

**Sheila Dempsey**
is a nursery teacher at
Guthrie CE Infant and Nursery
School in Calne, Wiltshire.

## Using the display
### Personal, social and emotional development
● Talk about how colours make us feel. Do the children associate feelings of warmth or danger with reds and oranges, or feelings of calm with blues and greens?
● Make a floor book using the children's paintings. Annotate their remarks regarding how they feel about their work.

### Communication, language and literacy
● Read *Mouse Paint* by Ellen Stoll Walsh (Orchard Books).

### Mathematical development
● Ask the children to sort coloured resources from around your setting.
● Make a chart to find the children's favourite colours or the colours of their front doors.

### Knowledge and understanding of the world
● Collect different-coloured fruits. Encourage the children to predict what colour each fruit will be inside.
● Visit a DIY store to look at the paint-mixing machine.

### Physical development
● Take the children for a walk and encourage them to look for colours in the environment.
● Pretend to be the parts of your colour-mixing machine. Make up a movement sequence and work together to be cogs and colours.

### Creative development
● When the children are secure with primary and secondary colours, make a 'tone colour machine', adding white and black to the primary colours.

# The sunshine tree

**Help to boost the children's self esteem and reward kind deeds by working together to create this beautiful display**

© Janet Holt

**Stepping Stone:** relate and make attachments to members of their group (PSED).
**Early Learning Goal:** form good relationships with adults and peers (PSED).
**Group size:** whole group.

## What you need

Blue, brown and white backing paper; white A4 paper; yellow, brown and green paint; paintbrushes; printing shapes; green tissue paper; yellow gummed paper; thin card circles; laminating materials; marker pen; computer (if available); laminated card name badges (one for each child in your group); pegs; basket.

## What to do

● Begin by talking about behaviour with the children. Encourage them to think about times when they have been helpful.
● Make a list of their suggestions. These might include listening, being kind, tidying up or sharing.
● Explain to the children that you are going to work together to make a display that will help to show how you help each other every day.

● Back a wall or board with dark blue paper and ask the children to help you to tear out the shape of a tree trunk and branches from dark brown paper. Attach to the board to make a tree.
● Ask the children to make some rolling hills at the bottom of the display by printing yellow and green shapes on to sheets of white paper.
● When dry, attach to the display. Add crumpled green tissue to represent grass.
● Make a border of bright suns, containing words from your list of helpful things. Invite the children to add sun rays by tearing and sticking on strips of gummed paper.
● Show the children your basket of name badges, and help each child to find their own badge. Explain that, each day, you are going to decide together who has done something helpful, and that child will be able to peg their name on to the sunshine tree.

**Janet Holt**
is a nursery teacher at
Palacefields CP School, Runcorn.

## Using the display
### Personal, social and emotional development

● Visit a garden nursery and choose your own sunshine tree, such as willow, to grow at your setting. Look after it together and watch it grow through the year.
● Include the children's families and friends on the display tree.

### Communication, language and literacy

● During circle time, invite individuals to suggest someone who has helped them today.
● Read *Tattybogle* by Sandra Horn and Ken Brown (Hodder) and talk about how the sun, wind and rain helped Tattybogle to grow into a beautiful tree.

### Mathematical development

● Use the display for counting activities. How many badges are on the tree today? How many boys? How many girls?
● Mark the children's heights on the tree. Who is the tallest?

### Knowledge and understanding of the world

● Find out about the different animals and birds that live in or under trees, and that eat the fruit from them.
● Make simple family trees, including friends and pets!

### Physical development

● Pretend to grow your own trees. Invite some children to be shoots and some to be gardeners. What do the gardeners need to do to help the shoots grow?

### Creative development

● Make individual sunshine-tree pictures by sponge-printing trunks and blowing runny paint for branches. When dry, add bright sunshines using yellow pastels.

# Deep blue sea

**Experiment with different construction techniques to make this interactive display full of colourful sea creatures**

**Stepping Stones:** construct with a purpose in mind using a variety of resources (KUW); manipulate materials to achieve a planned effect (PD).

**Early Learning Goals:** select the tools and techniques they need to shape, assemble and join the materials they are using (KUW); handle tools, objects, construction and malleable materials safely and with increasing control (PD).

**Group size:** whole group or pairs.

## What you need

Shoeboxes; different types of blue paper; sticks; paddles; string; glue; scissors; card; double-sided tape; fabric; turquoise backing paper; lettering; computer; sea-life books.

## What to do

● If possible, visit a sea-life centre with the children prior to creating your display. Back at your setting, share books and talk about the things that you saw during your visit.

● Invite the children to make a display of the creatures and plants that they saw.

● Give each child a shoebox and ask them to tear strips of blue, green and silver paper to stick inside for a water effect.

● While the boxes are drying, encourage the children, in pairs, to plan which animals they would like to put in their aquariums.

● Demonstrate how to use various techniques to attach the animals to the boxes so that they move. For example, attach crab shapes on sticks so that they can be moved backwards and forwards, glue jellyfish shapes on to paddles so that they can dangle from the top of the boxes, or suspend fish from lengths of string.

● Invite the children to select the materials and tools they will need to make their animals. Provide outlines for them to copy if necessary, including an octopus, sharks, rays, fish, crabs, and anemones.

● Cover a display board with turquoise backing paper and add a contrasting border.

● Mount the title for your display in blue circles to represent bubbles in the water.

● Staple the finished aquariums in random positions.

● Encourage the children to use the computer to type their own labels, then let them trim and mount the labels independently.

● Add a table covered with blue shimmering fabric in front of the display. Include underwater play creatures and books.

## Using the display

### Personal, social and emotional development

● Discuss caring for tropical fish in aquariums.

● Talk to the children about the importance of keeping safe near open water.

### Communication, language and literacy

● Take the children to a sea-life centre, then make a shared non-fiction book about your visit.

● Create posters showing the different animals and fish that live under the sea.

### Mathematical development

● Let the children use shape sponges to print pictures of sea creatures to add to the display.

● Count the different animals on your display. Make a graph to present the information.

### Knowledge and understanding of the world

● Use a Pixie dressed as a submarine to navigate a journey underwater.

● Invite the children to roll a dice on a floor map of the world and find the correct type of animal to place on the spot where it lands, depending on whether it is water or land.

### Creative development

● Use musical instruments to compose watery underwater music.

● Make observational drawings of shells and fish.

### Physical development

● Create a dance to your underwater music and let the children pretend to be different underwater creatures.

● Use junk materials to make a large-scale submarine.

**Louise Clark** is a Foundation Stage manager.

# Take a taste

**Sample different foods from around the world as you put together this colourful display**

© Estelle Corke

**Stepping Stone:** show curiosity, observe and manipulate objects (KUW).
**Early Learning Goal:** Investigate objects and materials by using all of their senses as appropriate (KUW).
**Group size:** whole group.

## What you need

Display board; dark blue mounting paper; small world flags; coloured sugar paper; green shredded paper; glue; spreaders; blue balloons; green paint; staple gun (adult use); globe (Early Learning Centre supplies a child-friendly picture globe, tel: 08705 352352); samples of food and packaging from around the world, such as Japanese miso soup, Indian sweets, Mexican fajitas, French croissants, Chinese rice and German sauerkraut. Include familiar items, such as tea-bags and cocoa powder.

## What to do

● Check for food allergies and dietary requirements.
● Begin by exploring the foods that you have collected. Encourage the children to describe the different foods. What do they smell like? Take a small sample of each and describe the texture. What does the sauerkraut feel like? What about the rice? Invite the children to sample the food.

● Now look at the packaging. Does it say where the foods have come from?
● Look at the globe and find the countries where your food samples came from.
● Invite the children to help you to make a display showing the different foods that we enjoy from around the world.
● Cover a display board with dark blue paper. Make a border from small flags.
● Cut a large circle from pale blue sugar paper. Let the children stick on green shredded paper to represent land in the blue sea. When dry, attach to the board.
● Stick letters to form the words 'Around the world' on to small globe shapes, then attach them to the board.
● Blow up the blue balloons. Encourage the children to use green paint to design their own globes. Suspend above the display.
● Invite the children to display the food packaging in front of the display. Add appropriate labels and the children's comments about the food.

**Caroline Jackson** and **Collette Miller** are nursery nurses in Manchester.

## Using the display

### Personal, social and emotional development
● Let the children dress up in national costumes from around the world.
● Set up a role-play world food restaurant.

### Communication, language and literacy
● Add question cards to the display, such as 'What is your favourite food?' and 'Which food do you not like?' to promote discussion.
● Look at the different types of print that is used on the packaging. Find examples of different languages.

### Mathematical development
● Sort the food packaging using different criteria, such as contents, colour and size.
● Place some balance scales on a table next to the display. Let the children weigh the foodstuffs using non-standard measures.

### Knowledge and understanding of the world
● Find out about different types of cutlery that is used in other countries.
● Follow simple recipes from around the world to make food such as pizza, barfi and kebab.

### Physical development
● Talk about healthy foods and exercising.
● Use different types of food packages for modelling.

### Creative development
● Design your own food labels for imaginary food!
● Look at the designs of flags from some of the countries around the world.

# Scare those crows!

**Bring the countryside indoors with this colourful display of fields, wheat and scarecrows**

**Stepping Stone:** make constructions, collages, paintings and drawings (CD).
**Early Learning Goal:** explore colour, texture, shape, form and space in two or three dimensions (CD).
**Group size:** whole group, small groups and individuals.

## What you need

*Tattybogle* by Sandra Horn and Ken Brown (Hodder Children's Books); gold, green and orange paper; white card; crow and mouse shapes; black sugar paper and crêpe paper; wheat; fabric scraps; fake fur; small flowerpots; Plasticine; lollipop sticks; red tissue paper; glue; green fabric; hessian; sequins; paint and painting equipment; felt-tipped pens; table.

© Louise Clark

## What you do

● Share the book together.
● Cover the display area with gold paper. Add green border and wheat along the bottom.
● Cut out a large cardboard scarecrow and invite the children to collage it with fabric scraps, paint the face and hair and add facial features. Staple the scarecrow across a corner to give a free-standing effect.
● Ask the children to paint individual scarecrows. Cut them out, mount on black and orange paper and staple to the display.
● Let the children collage fake fur on to mouse shapes.
● Invite the children to collage black crêpe feathers on to crow shapes. Add yellow beaks and sequin eyes. When dry, cut a horizontal slit across the middle and concentina black paper as wings to thread through the slit. Staple the crows and mice to the display.
● Cut out circles from black sugar paper and glue red tissue-paper petals at the edge on the reverse to make poppies.
● Place a table in front of the display and cover with green fabric and hessian.

● Help the children to make more scarecrows, cutting out triangles for bodies, circles for faces and rectangles for hats.
● Encourage the children to collage the hats and bodies with fabric. Show them how to make a cross with lollipop sticks and attach the shapes to the sticks make a scarecrow. Let the children add details to the faces with felt-tipped pens.
● Ask the children to put Plasticine in the flowerpots, push the scarecrows in and place them on the table.
● Add labels, such as, 'How many crows can you see?'.
● Make a heading from white card mounted on to black. Collage the letters with fabric.

**Louise Clark**
is a Foundation Stage manager.

## Using the display
### Personal social and emotional development

● Discuss the seasons of the year and the different clothes that we wear to keep us warm, cool and dry.
● Tattybogle was lost as he was blown away by the wind. Ask the children if they have ever lost anything. Did they find it? How did they feel when they lost something then found it again?

### Communication, language and literacy

● Invite the children to trace a picture of a scarecrow and make up a name for it.
● Make a group poster of directions to find Tattybogle.

### Mathematical development

● Create a scarecrow from 2-D and 3-D shapes.
● Use the display as an opportunity for counting.

### Knowledge and understanding of the world

● Talk about the changing seasons and weather at different times of the year.
● Use the scarecrow to encourage the children to become familiar with different parts of the body. Look at similarities and differences.

### Creative development

● Learn songs and poems about scarecrows.
● Try out different painting skills to create a wheatfield on black sugar paper.

### Physical development

● Develop a scarecrow dance through the year.
● Invite the children to play 'What's the Time, Mr Wolf?' with Mr Scarecrow and little crows.

# Growing the family tree

**Bring families together with this attractive display showing lots of different family members**

© Gaynor Berry

**Stepping Stone:** show interest in the lives of people familiar to them (KUW).

**Early Learning Goal:** find out about past and present events in their own lives, and in those of their families and other people they know (KUW).

**Group size:** small groups for discussion; whole group to make display.

## What you need

Bucket; sand; long twigs; card; coloured paint; painting equipment; aprons; glue; string; green tissue paper; books and pictures of family groups; small-world toys representing families.

## What to do

● Show the family pictures to the children and invite them to talk about their own families.

● Help the children to fill the bucket with sand and push the twigs into it.

● Let the children cover the bucket with green tissue paper cut to look like grass.

● Cut out different-shaped card leaves and let the children sponge paint the leaves.

● Invite the children to paint a picture of a member of their family, then mount it on their leaf.

● On the reverse of the leaves, help the children to write who the person is.

● Make a hole in each leaf, thread some string through and attach it to the tree.

● Discuss the small-world figures and display them on a table next to the display. Make labels explaining who they represent.

● Add the books and pictures to the display.

● Ask parents to bring in family photographs. Share these with the group and display with parents' permission.

**Jenny Etheredge**
is the Pre-School Leader at Thames
Pre-School in Cricklade, Wiltshire.

## Using the display
### Personal, social and emotional development

● Discuss friendship and what it means to the children. What is a good friend?

● Invite a parent with a baby to talk to the children about caring for babies and the equipment that they need.

### Communication, language and literacy

● Invite the children to tell the group what they call different family members, such as 'Granny', 'Grandma' and 'Nan'. Use these names to label the display.

● Discuss family outings. Where do the children go with their families?

### Mathematical development

● Invite the children to put the family figures in size order.

● Let the children use tape measures to measure each other. Plot the results on a height chart.

### Knowledge and understanding of the world

● Let the children take photographs of their family and display them.

● Celebrate 'Grandparent's Day' together each year.

### Physical development

● Play a version of 'Simon says'. For example, 'Simon says jump up and down, if you have a sister'.

● Discuss the different physical needs of family members – what they eat and how active they are. Can the children suggest why?

### Creative development

● Make finger puppets of family members to use for role-play and story-telling.

● Let the children play out different family roles in the home corner.

# Setting safety

**Help the children to think about safe play and practices with this attractive display**

© Gill Birch

**Stepping Stone:** value and contribute to own well-being and self-control (PSED).
**Early Learning Goal:** work as part of a group or class, taking turns and sharing fairly, understanding that there needs to be agreed values and codes of behaviour for groups of people, including adults and children, to work together harmoniously (PSED).
**Group size:** whole group, followed by small group and individual work.

## What you need
Display board; white, yellow and black card; black pens; camera; photographic paper; string; PVA glue; yellow material; books on safety, electricity and science; computer.

## What to do
● Discuss the need to be safe at your setting.
● Draw up a list together of ways to be safe, reflecting issues specific to your setting.
● Take some photographs of the children, with parental consent, carrying out these actions safely around your setting.

● Display the title 'Be safe' with mounted and labelled photographs showing safe practices.
● Let the children draw their own pictures on circles, illustrating all these safe actions.
● Make labels, using a computer, describing each picture so their meaning is clear.
● Mount the pictures and labels, and display them around the list of rules for being safe.
● Finish the display with drawings by children of themselves with very large smiles. This is to show how much better everyone will feel if they are playing in a safe and caring environment.
● Mount the faces on black card and add to the display as a border.
● Add the books and videos about being safe, careful and considerate of others on a table in front of the display.

**Gill Birch**
is a nursery teacher in Chester.

## Using the display
### Personal, social and emotional development
● Ask the children how they feel when they are safe, happy and unhurt. Consider possible dangers in the setting and at home. Talk about how they would feel if they were affected.
● Discuss how the children travel to the setting and how to be safe.

### Communication, language and literacy
● Create concertina leaflets with photographs of the children being safe (with parental permission).
● Produce safety posters for the setting, reminding everyone to behave appropriately.

### Mathematical development
● Encourage the children to line up in a safe, orderly manner. Introduce and discuss ordinal language, such as 'first' and 'second'.
● Develop mathematical language relating to speed, pace and timing, such as 'fast' and 'slow'.

### Knowledge and understanding of the world
● Discuss types of equipment that use electricity and the rules for using them safely.
● Investigate how to be safe in and near different environments, including tall buildings, woods, water and fire.

### Physical development
● Encourage the children to ride bikes safely, wearing helmets and protective pads.
● Set up a role-play road crossing and practise 'The Green Cross Code'.

### Creative development
● Display handprints by sinks to remind children to wash hands.
● Create footprint tracks around the setting to encourage walking instead of running.

# Castle in the clouds

**Watch your own magic beanstalks grow up to the clouds with this stunning interactive display**

© Gaynor Berry

## Using the display

### Personal, social and emotional development

● Find out about the best way to care for your beans as they grow.
● Work together to measure your beanstalks each week.

### Communication, language and literacy

● Learn the names of the different parts of your beanstalks.
● Retell the story and sequence the events in the correct order.

### Mathematical development

● Measure the beanstalks using other non-standard measures such as bricks or toy cars.
● Record the growth of the beans on a simple chart.

### Knowledge and understanding of the world

● Talk about the changes that happen as the plants grow.
● Record the beans' growth using a digital camera.

### Physical development

● Mime the movements for throwing the beans, the beanstalk growing, Jack climbing, Jack tiptoeing to the giant's castle and the giant lumbering down the beanstalk. Put a sequence of movements together to tell the story.

### Creative development

● Cook and eat different types of beans.
● Use percussion instruments to create sounds for the characters and events in the story.

**Stepping Stones:** use size language such as 'big' and 'little'; order two items by length or height (MD).

**Early Learning Goal:** use language such as 'circle' or 'bigger' to describe the shape and size of solids and flat shapes (MD).

**Group size:** whole group to make display; groups of four or five to grow individual beans.

## What you need

Display board; blue frieze paper; painting paper; sponges; white tissue paper; paint in assorted colours; dry sand; glue; scissors; drawing materials; paintbrushes; string; plant pots; soil; beans.

## What to do

● Remind the children about the story of 'Jack and the Beanstalk'.
● Tell the children that you would like them to help you make an interactive display that will grow every day!
● Cover the board in blue frieze paper. Invite the children to create fluffy clouds by painting large white cloud shapes, then sticking screwed-up white tissue paper over the shape. Sponge-paint over the tissue with white and pale blue paint. Arrange the clouds on the backing paper.
● Invite the children to help draw a castle shape and cover it with yellow paint, mixed with sand. Paint on the windows and a door, and mount it on top of the clouds.
● At the bottom of the board let the children either paint or print grass.
● Place the beanstalk pots at the base of the display, with a gap between each pot. Run a string up the board from the grass to the castle. The beans will grow up the string towards the clouds.
● Ask the children to make handprints and cut them out. Number these and mount them beside the display to use as a non-standard measure.
● Finally, plant the beans and place the pots at the base of each string.
● When your display is finished, put up questions to encourage adult interaction and extend the children's learning.

**Ruth Goodman**
is a nursery teacher at De Havilland Primary School in Hatfield.

# Underground foods

**Create a colourful display to help the children learn about foods that grow beneath the ground.**

*© Derek Cooknell*

**Stepping Stone:** show an interest in the world in which they live (KUW).
**Early Learning Goal:** observe, find out about and identify features in the place they live and the natural world (KUW).
**Group size:** whole group.

## What you need

*The Enormous Turnip* (*Favourite Tales* series, Ladybird Books); neutral backing paper; white border paper; purple and orange fabric scraps; string; paints; cardboard 'comb'; sponge; tissue paper; toothbrush; potatoes, carrots, onions and beetroot; plastic 'grass'; 'hyacinth' jar; tinned carrots; dried onions; pickled beetroot; carrot and beetroot seed packets; soup and sauce mixes; empty frozen vegetable bags; gardening books; recipe books.

## What to do

● Share the story of *The Enormous Turnip* with the children.
● Talk about other foods that grow underground and suggest that the children help to make a display to show these.
● Cover the display board with neutral backing paper and invite a group of children to sponge print it using brown and blue paint to represent the soil and the sky.
● Let the children use a toothbrush to splatter paint to add texture.

● Cut a border with a scalloped edge and let the children use potatoes and carrots, cut in half, to print patterns. Staple the border to the display board.
● Cut out the outline of a large beetroot from sugar paper. Invite the children to choose appropriate colours to paint the outline. When it is dry, encourage them to add texture by gluing on fabric strips in different shades of purple.
● Create tiny hair-like 'roots' by dipping string in purple paint. Invite the children to make large bushy 'leaves' from scrunched-up green tissue paper.
● Let the children use a similar method to make a carrot from orange fabric.
●Create an onion by swirling thick brown paint using a cardboard comb.
● Ask the children to make beetles, worms and stones from collage materials.
● Attach labels to indicate names, position, size and shape.
● Cover the table with the plastic grass and display carrots, onions and beetroot, together with the seed packets, soup and sauce mixes, empty frozen vegetable bags, gardening books and recipe books.

**Jean Evans**
is an early years
consultant and author.

## Using the display
### Personal, social and emotional development
● Grow beetroot and carrot tops and ask the children to water them daily. Grow potatoes in a bucket.
● Encourage turn-taking, sharing and concentration skills by preparing vegetables for home-made soup.

### Communication, language and literacy
● Read the traditional stories *The Enormous Turnip* and *Jack and the Beanstalk* (both *Favourite Tales* series, Ladybird Books). Talk about the children's experiences of growing vegetables.
● Make observational drawings of vegetables and invite the children to label the roots, stalk and leaves.

### Mathematical development
● Sort a box of mixed vegetables into different types. Count how many of each kind there are.
● Make a number line from 1 to 10 showing different types of vegetables.

### Knowledge and understanding of the world
● Let the children experiment with the different conditions that are needed for growth, for example, keep some seeds in the dark and others in the light, and water some seeds and leave others dry. Observe and discuss your findings.

### Physical development
● Invite the children to re-enact the story of 'The Enormous Turnip', emphasising the movements needed to pull up the huge turnip.
● Let the children use a range of tools, such as small spades, spoons, trowels and forks, to sow seeds in plant pots and decide which are the best for the task.

### Creative development
● Encourage the children to move to appropriate music and pretend to be roots stretching down into the soil and stalks growing up in the light.

# In the jungle

**Bring the jungle into your setting with this exciting and colourful display**

© Gill Birch

**Stepping Stone:** show curiosity and interest by facial expression, movement or sound (KUW).
**Early Learning Goal:** investigate objects and materials by using all of their senses as appropriate (KUW).
**Group size:** whole group.

## What you need

*Rumble in the Jungle* by Giles Andreae and David Wojtowycz (Orchard Books); green backing paper or display board; white paper; white card; different-coloured poster paint; safety scissors; green crêpe paper; wooden dowel sticks; PVA glue; green tissue paper; newspaper; sticky tape; green netting; marbling inks; green camouflage material; toy snake; sponges; trays; books and videos about the jungle.

## What to do

● Share the book *Rumble in the Jungle* with the children.
● Talk about how the jungle is made up of many different types of plants, trees, bushes, leaves and flowers. Point out that most of these will not be seen in gardens or local parks.
● Explain to the children that they are going to make a display to show a jungle environment. Discuss the range of colours and different shapes that you would like them to include.

● Cover the display board with green backing paper and add green netting or camouflage material to emphasise the jungle effect.
● Give the children a sheet of paper and invite them to use a variety of paint effects, such as marbling, stippling and sponge printing, encouraging them to fill the whole sheet.
● Ask the children to draw different leaf shapes on the printed sheet and encourage them to cut out the shapes out carefully.
● Help the children to twist green crêpe paper to create vines. Alternatively, twist newspaper and mask with tape, then paint it green for a different effect.
● Mount the vines and leaves on the wall. If possible, continue with the leaves on to the ceiling to create a 3-D effect.
● Invite the children to paint large, brightly-coloured flower heads on to pieces of white card.
● Help the children to cover pieces of dowel with green tissue paper to create flower stems. Attach them to the display with PVA glue and add the flower heads to them.
● Create dragonflies and butterflies to finish the jungle effect.
● Set up a table below the display with a toy snake or similar jungle animal, books and videos about the jungle and different jungle animals for everyone to enjoy.

## Using the display
### Personal social and emotional development
● Discuss the need to care and look after plants and the environment.
● Consider wildlife that live in different habitats and how they need to adapt in order to survive.

### Communication, language and literacy
● Ask the children to write poems about the thins that they might see on a walk through the jungle.
● Encourage the children to describe trees, plants and leaves that they can see at your setting.

### Mathematical development
● Put the toy snake in different places on the display and encourage the children to use the words 'above', 'below', 'next to' and so on.
● Compare different-sized leaves, using language such as 'longer than' and 'shorter than'.

### Knowledge and understanding of the world
● Take the children to visit a safari park, with parental permission.
● Identify the animals that live in the jungle and discuss the type of things that they eat.

### Physical development
● Take an imaginary walk through the jungle, discussing the different vegetation that you might encounter and the animals you might meet.
● Let the children make leaves from clay, then paint and glaze them.

### Creative development
● Use musical instruments to add sounds to the story, such as crinkling paper for walking through leaves.
● Make a group wall hanging on hessian, using felt and other fabrics for trees, leaves and flowers. Sew on twigs to look like branches.

**Gill Birch**
is a Foundation
Stage teacher.

# Holiday fun for bear

**Take teddy on a worldwide tour with this fantastic display**

**Stepping Stones:** show an interest in the world in which they live; express feelings about a significant personal event (KUW).

**Early Learning Goals:** observe, find out about and identify features in the place they live and the natural world (KUW); begin to know about their own cultures and beliefs and those of other people (KUW).

**Group size:** individual work on computer; small groups for artwork and written work.

## What you need
Large wall map of the world; teddy bear; computer; printer; computer program such as *My First Amazing World Explorer CD-ROM Activity Pack* (Dorling Kindersley) (optional); blue and green paper; cut-out speech bubbles; books about the world; holiday brochures; bear template; writing and colouring materials; display board; blue backing paper; yellow paper; glue.

## What to do
● Cover a display board with blue backing paper and mount a world map in the centre.
● Show the children the teddy bear and explain that he would like to go on holiday.
● Invite the children to tell you what they think makes a good holiday.
● Look at the world map together and talk about visiting different countries on holiday.
● Look at the green areas and blue areas on the map and discuss what each colour represents.
● Give the children some blue and green paper. Invite them to make a map by tearing pieces of green paper to look like islands and stick them on to the blue sea. Use these as a border for your display board.

● Let the children use the CD-ROM to travel the world and collect information. Invite them to print out where they would like to send the bear on holiday. Alternatively, let them look at the world map and choose a destination.
● Encourage the children to give a reason for their choice, then help them to write in a speech bubble why they think the bear would like to go to their chosen destination.
● Give each child a bear template and encourage them to 'dress' it in appropriate holiday clothes.
● Position the children's bears in the correct position on the map.
● Mount the printed information and speech bubbles on to yellow paper and position them around the world map.
● Add the title 'Holiday fun for bear'.
● Place a selection of books about the world and holiday brochures, and a teddy bear (with a small suitcase, if possible) in front of the display.

## Using the display
### Personal, social and emotional development
● Talk about the things that people do on holiday. Discuss how people's ideas about holidays vary, depending on what they like to do. Invite the children to suggest a variety of holidays.
● Encourage the children to talk about how we can recall holidays by collecting memories in different ways, such as writing in diaries, keeping postcards and souvenirs and taking photographs.

### Communication, language and literacy
● Turn your role-play area into an airport and let the children pretend to go abroad on holiday.
● Make a pretend passport and fill in all the relevant details.
● Let the children write and send a postcard to a friend.

### Mathematical development
● Make a graph showing the things that the children like to do on their holidays.
● Encourage the children to count holiday objects in a suitcase.

### Knowledge and understanding of the world
● Invite the children to use a programmable toy to travel around a large world floor map.
● Look at suitable clothes for different climates.
● Discuss places of interest that people visit on holiday.

### Physical development
● Encourage the children to learn a traditional dance, such as the Irish Jig or the Spanish Flamenco.

### Creative development
● Draw a selection of swimwear and encourage the children to paint a design on them.
● Listen to a variety of music from different countries.

**Louise Clark**
is a Foundation Stage manager.

# It's time for a story

**There's no reason to forget when it's time for the next activity with this bright and colourful display**

**Stepping Stone:** begin to differentiate between past and present (KUW).
**Early Learning Goal:** find out about past and present events in their own lives, and in those of their families and other people they know (KUW).
**Group size:** whole group.

## What you need

Display board; table; dark blue backing paper; yellow, red and black sugar paper; black card; computer and printer; blue and white paper; child scissors; glue; stapler; Blu-Tack; paper fastener; crayons; two red clothes pegs; hand bell; collection of old clocks and watches.

## What to do

● As this display is interactive, ensure that you set it up at the correct level for the children.
● Cover a display board with blue backing paper.
● Create a border using yellow sugar paper.
● Invite a group of children to create two sets of large, colourful numbers from 1 to 12 on a computer, by changing the size, font and colours.
● Help the children to print out the numbers and cut them out.
● Ask the children to arrange the numbers down the right- and left-hand sides of the display using Blu-Tack.
● Draw a large watch face on a sheet of white paper and help the children to write the numbers 1 to 12 around the outside. Mount on to a slightly larger circle of red sugar paper. Glue this to the centre of the display.
● Cut two watch hands from black sugar paper. Use a paper fastener to attach these to a small circle of black card. Glue around the perimeter of the circle and fix to the centre of the watch face, making sure that the hands turn easily.
● Ask the children to help you make a giant watch strap from yellow sugar paper and adjoin it to the watch face.
● As the children work, encourage the use of time language.

© Lynda Murray

● Invite all the children to draw a self-portrait on to a piece of white paper. Let them cut them out carefully and use them to decorate the watchstrap.
● Encourage a group of children to draw pictures of the different activities that they sometimes carry out during the session, such as storytime, outdoor play, snack time and so on. On each drawing, display a small clock face showing the time that the activity usually takes place.
● Glue two clothes pegs on to the display board under the watch and attach an activity drawing.
● Arrange a collection of old watches and clocks on a table together with the rest of the drawings.
● Hang a bell from the display and let the children take turns, in pairs, to ring the bell when it is a transition time. Tell them the next activity and ask them to select the correct drawing, hang it from the clothes pegs and change the hands on the watch to match those on the activity drawing.

## Using the display
### Personal, social and emotional development

● Ask the children to work together co-operatively when selecting and changing the activity during transition time.

### Communication, language and literacy

● Hide a ticking clock from the display around your setting and encourage the children to search for it by responding to simple instructions and using listening skills.

### Mathematical development

● Play the 'Just a minute' challenge. Using various clocks from the display, ask the children to count how many beads they can thread or how many bricks they can make into a tower in one minute.

### Knowledge and understanding of the world

● Make a sand clock by piercing a small hole in the cap of a plastic bottle. Half fill another bottle with fine sand and leave off the cap. Tape the two bottle tops together. Turn the clock upside-down and see how long it takes for the sand to fall through.

### Physical development

● Encourage the children to pump their arms up and down, kick a leg forwards and backwards, or jump up and down as they say 'tick tock' to a regular beat.

### Creative development

● Make 'bubble clocks' by bubble-printing bright colours on to white paper plates. Write the numbers around the outside of the 'clock' and add hands using paper fasteners.

**Beverley Michael**
is an early years writer.

# Chapter 4
# Songs

You don't have to be a music
expert to bring the songs in this
chapter to life! Children will love
joining in with the actions to
these fun songs, all set
to favourite traditional tunes.

# All about me

## (To the tune of 'Polly Put the Kettle on')

F          G          C

1. Now I'm big I count to ten,     fin - gers toes and back a - gain.

F          G     C     F

One, two, three, four, five, six, se - ven. Eight, nine, ten.

## Verses

**2** I can play with girls and boys,
Make new friends and share my toys.
Stand on one leg, turn around,
Sit on the ground.

**3** I try hard to get things right,
I sleep soundly through the night.
Washing hands and getting dressed,
I try my best.

**4** Soon I'll learn to tie my shoes,
Stand up bravely, share my news.
Sit quite still and wait my turn,
These things I'll learn.

© **Sanchia Sewell**

## Using the song

Add appropriate actions to accompany
each verse:
**1** Count on fingers or toes from one to
ten.
**2** Link arms with child standing alongside
to represent friends. Stand on one leg,
turn around and sit down.
**3** Join hands together and rest head on
them to indicate sleeping. Pretend to
wash and dry hands and pull on jumpers.
**4** Bend down to tie shoes, stand up
straight and tall to share news, then end
by sitting down quietly.

© Louise Gardner

Creative play

# Father Christmas

## (To the tune of 'Frère Jacques')

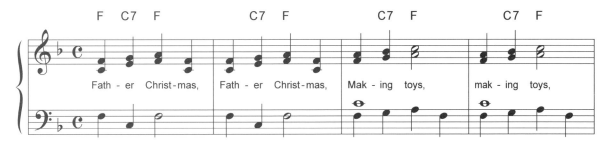

Fath - er Christ - mas, Fath - er Christ - mas, Mak - ing toys, mak - ing toys,

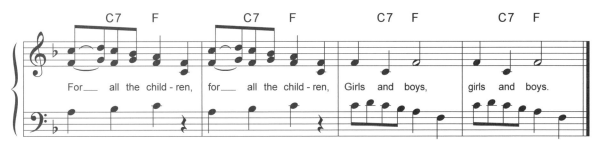

For__ all the child - ren, for__ all the child - ren, Girls and boys, girls and boys.

## Verses

**2** Father Christmas, Father Christmas,
Beard so white, beard so white.
See his reindeer flying,
See his reindeer flying,
Through the night,
Through the night.

**3** Father Christmas, Father Christmas,
On his sleigh, on his sleigh.
He is bringing presents,
He is bringing presents,
For Christmas day,
Christmas day.

**4** Father Christmas, Father Christmas,
We thank you, we thank you.
Thank you for the good things,
Thank you for the good things,
That you do,
That you do.

**© Faye Robertson**

## Using the song

Add appropriate actions to accompany each verse:
**1** Pretend to hammer as if making wooden toys.
**2** Stroke chin, indicating a long beard!
**3** Use one arm to show the sleigh flying through the night.
**4** Children point to themselves at 'we thank' and to an adult or another child at 'you'.

# The weather

## (To the tune of 'London Bridge is Falling Down')

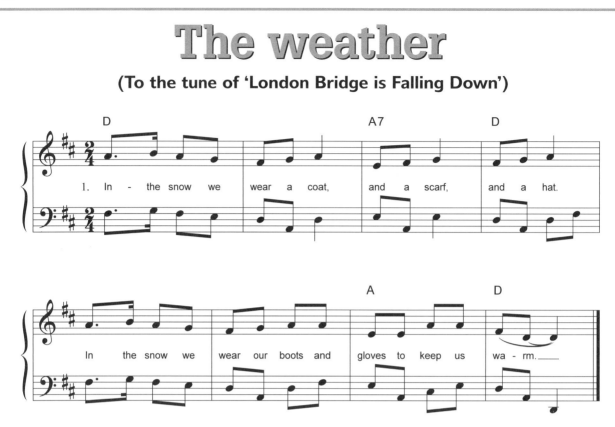

1. In - the snow we wear a coat, and a scarf, and a hat.

In the snow we wear our boots and gloves to keep us wa - rm.

## Verses

**2** In the rain we wear a mac,
wellington boots, splish splish splash.
In the rain our hair gets wet,
we put up our umbrellas.

**3** In the sun our skin may burn,
rub on cream, slap slap slap.
In the sun it's very bright,
we put on our sunglasses.

**4** In the wind we feel it blow,
on our face, on our clothes.
In the wind we fasten our coats
to keep us snug and warm.

© **Sally Scott**

# I'm a little snail

## (To the tune of 'Sing a Song of Sixpence')

1. I'm a lit-tle snail with a shell up-on my back. It's made of diff'-rent co-lours like white and brown and black. The co-lours make a pat-tern as pret-ty as can be, that's diff-rent from all o-ther snails and quite u-nique to me.

**Verses**

2 We are little spiders; we're spinning lots of webs.
We're spinning with our spinnerets and lots of silky threads.
Although each web looks different, the pattern stays the same,
First straight threads from the middle, then others going round.

**© Sanchia Sewell**

## Using the song

The first verse aims to show that by looking at patterns, we can detect differences in similar-shaped objects. If possible, collect some snail shells for the children to look at. Encourage them to notice the differences in the patterns and colours of each shell. Sing the first verse through a few times. The second verse explores the concept of following a basic pattern. Draw a big spider's web starting with straight lines radiating from a central point, then add the circles. Draw another, making it bigger (or smaller), and discuss how it differs from the first web, although you used the same methods to draw each one.

Sing the second verse through a few times, then let the children draw their own webs.

© Louise Gardner

# Do you know what time it is?

## (To the tune of 'Mary had a Little Lamb')

Do you know what time it is, Time it is, time it is? Do you know what time it is? Let us look and see.

*Pause to look at the clock*

Yes I know what time it is, Time it is, time it is. Yes I know what time it is, It is three o' clock.

© **Sally Scott**

### Using the song

Before singing the song, set the time of a large wall clock or cardboard clock to three o'clock.

Sing the song with the children, pausing in the middle to look at the clock. Help the children to work out what time it is.

Finish singing the song, adding the clock's time at the end of the verse. Invite the children to change the time on the clock by one hour and sing the song again with the correct time.

Let older children set the clock and sing the song to more complicated times.

© Derek Cooknell

# Who is wearing red today?

## (To the tune of 'Polly Put the Kettle On')

© Sally Scott

### Using the song

Take several large pieces of card, choosing colours that are being worn by the children. Familiarize the children with each colour name.

As you sing, hold up the first coloured card, substituting the appropriate colour into the verse. Ask the children to join hands and dance around in a circle.

Stop dancing at 'Please stand in the middle', and decide together who should stand in the middle. Continue singing, with the remaining children dancing around the group in the middle.

Ask the children to return to the circle. Repeat the song holding up a different-coloured card until everyone has had a turn at standing in the middle.

# Five hungry penguins

## (To the tune of 'Ten Green Bottles')

© Louise Gardner

## Verses

**2** Four hungry penguins standing by the sea.
Four hungry penguins standing by the sea.
And if one hungry penguin should catch a fish for tea,
There'll be three hungry penguins standing by the sea.

**3** Three hungry penguins standing by the sea...

**4** Two hungry penguins standing by the sea...

**5** One hungry penguin standing by the sea.
One hungry penguin standing by the sea.
And if that hungry penguin should catch a fish for tea,
There'll be no hungry penguins standing by the sea.

© **Sally Scott**

### Using the song

You can sing this song with any number of children; just alter the number of penguins in the first verse. Place a large blue sheet on the floor to represent the sea and add cardboard fish cut-outs. Ask the children to stand around the edge of the 'sea' and pretend to be penguins, with their feet pointing outwards and their arms by their sides. At the end of each verse, one child should jump into the 'sea', take a fish and move away. Repeat until everyone has a fish for tea!

# Look outside

## (To the tune of 'This Old Man')

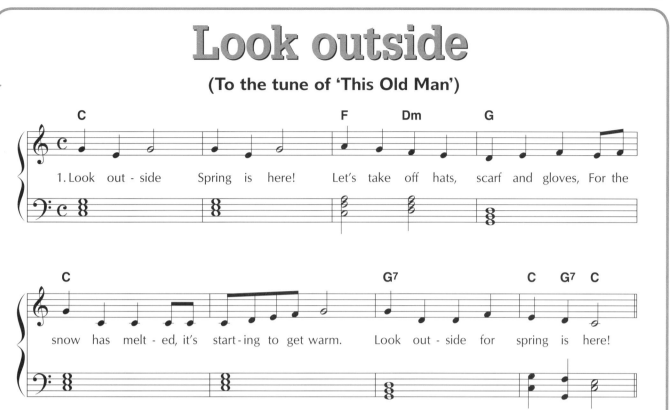

1. Look out - side Spring is here! Let's take off hats, scarf and gloves, For the

snow has melt - ed, it's start - ing to get warm. Look out - side for spring is here!

## Verses

**2** Look outside
Summer's here!
Let's take off our big warm coats,
For the sun is shining, it's very very hot.
Look outside for summer's here!

**3** Look outside
Autumn's here!
Let's put on our coats again,
For the sun has gone, it's windy and wet.
Look outside for autumn's here!

**4** Look outside
Winter's here!
Let's put on hats, scarves and gloves,
The snow is falling, it's icy and cold.
Look outside for winter's here!

© Sally Scott

## Using the song

Ask the children to bring in one or two items of clothing for each season. As you sing the song, practise putting on the clothing depending on the season that you are singing about. Accompany the verses with appropriate actions, such as mopping foreheads in the summer, and shivering and blowing hands in the winter!

# Ten shiny rockets

## (To the tune of 'Five Little Ducks Went Swimming One Day')

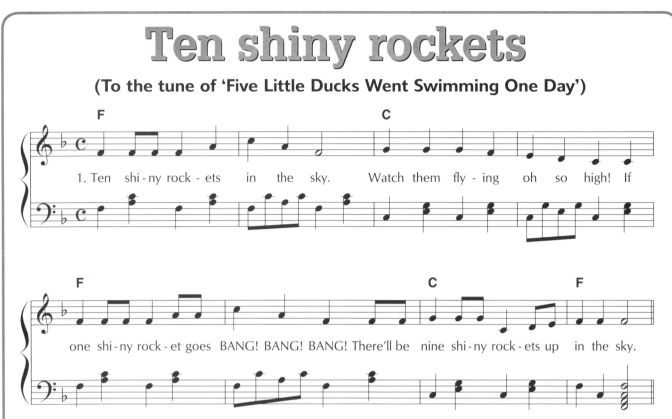

1. Ten shi-ny rock-ets in the sky. Watch them fly-ing oh so high! If one shi-ny rock-et goes BANG! BANG! BANG! There'll be nine shi-ny rock-ets up in the sky.

**Verses**

Nine shiny rockets in the sky.
Watch them flying oh so high!
If one shiny rocket goes BANG! BANG! BANG!
There'll be eight shiny rockets up in the sky.

Repeat verses until...

One shiny rocket in the sky.
Watch it flying oh so high!
If that shiny rocket goes BANG! BANG! BANG!
There'll be no shiny rockets left in the sky.

**© Sally Scott**

### Using the song

Invite ten children (or a number suitable for your group) to pretend to be rockets. Give the other children some percussion instruments. Ask the 'rockets' to run around the room as you all sing the song and play your instruments.

In each verse, on the words 'BANG! BANG! BANG!', ask the children to beat their instruments as loudly as possible. Choose one 'rocket' to sit down, leaving one less rocket for the next verse.

# Helping Granny and Grandad

## (To the tune of 'London Bridge is Falling Down')

1. I help Gran - ny sweep the floor, sweep the floor, sweep the floor.

I help Gran - ny sweep the floor when I vi - sit.____

### Verses

**2** help Grandad cut the grass,
Cut the grass, cut the grass.
I help Grandad cut the grass,
When I visit.

**3** help Granny wash the car,
Wash the car, wash the car.
I help Granny wash the car,
When I visit.

**4** help Grandad bake a cake,
Bake a cake, bake a cake.
I help Grandad bake a cake,
When I visit.

© Louise Gardner

### Using the song

While singing the song with the children, mime the following actions:

**Verse 1:** sweeping actions
**Verse 2:** mowing the lawn
**Verse 3:** washing the car with a sponge
**Verse 4:** stirring the cake mixture in a bowl.

Make up your own verses by asking the children to think of other things they can do to help their grandparents or elderly relatives.

# Cross the road

## (To the tune of 'Here We Go Round the Mulberry Bush')

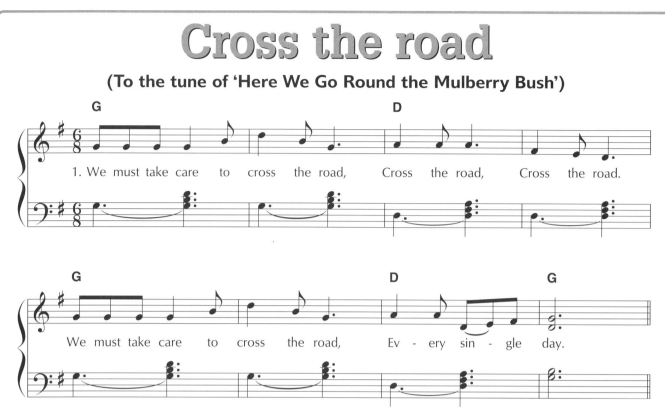

1. We must take care to cross the road, Cross the road, Cross the road.

We must take care to cross the road, Ev - ery sin - gle day.

## Verses

**2** Stop at the kerb and look both ways,
Look both ways, look both ways.
Stop at the kerb and look both ways,
Before we cross the road.

**3** Listen for cars and look again,
Look again, look again.
Listen for cars and look again,
Is it safe to cross?

**4** If it is safe we walk across,
Walk across, walk across.
If it is safe we walk across,
Safely over the road.

© **Sally Scott**

© Louise Gardner

## Using the song

While singing the song, mime the
actions described in each verse.
Pretend there's a road in the centre of
the room.
**Verse 1:** invite the children to stand
on one side of the 'road'.
**Verse 2:** look both ways while
singing the verse.
**Verse 3:** hold hands up to ears, as if
listening, and look both ways again.
**Verse 4:** all join hands and walk
across the 'road'.

# Let's all plant a magic bean in the ground

## (To the the tune of 'If You're Happy and You Know It')

1. Let's all plant a ma - gic bean in the ground. Let's all

plant a ma - gic bean in the ground. Let's all dig to make a hole and

plant the ma - gic bean. Let's all plant a ma - gic bean in the ground.

### Verses

**2** Let's all water the magic bean and watch it grow.
Let's all water the magic bean and watch it grow.
Watch it sprouting from the ground,
Stretching high up to the sky.
Let's all water the magic bean and watch it grow.

**3** Let's all climb the magic beanstalk to the top.
Let's all climb the magic beanstalk to the top.
Let's all climb up branch by branch,
Stretching high up to the sky.
Let's all climb the magic beanstalk to the top.

**© Sally Scott**

### Using the song
While singing the song, mime the actions described in each verse.

**Verse 1:** Kneel on the ground and dig to plant the bean.
**Verse 2:** Still on the ground, pretend to pour water over the bean, then pretend to be the bean sprouting from the ground and stretching high up into the sky.
**Verse 3:** Use climbing and stretching actions to climb the beanstalk.

# Growing every day

## (To the tune of 'Jelly on a Plate')

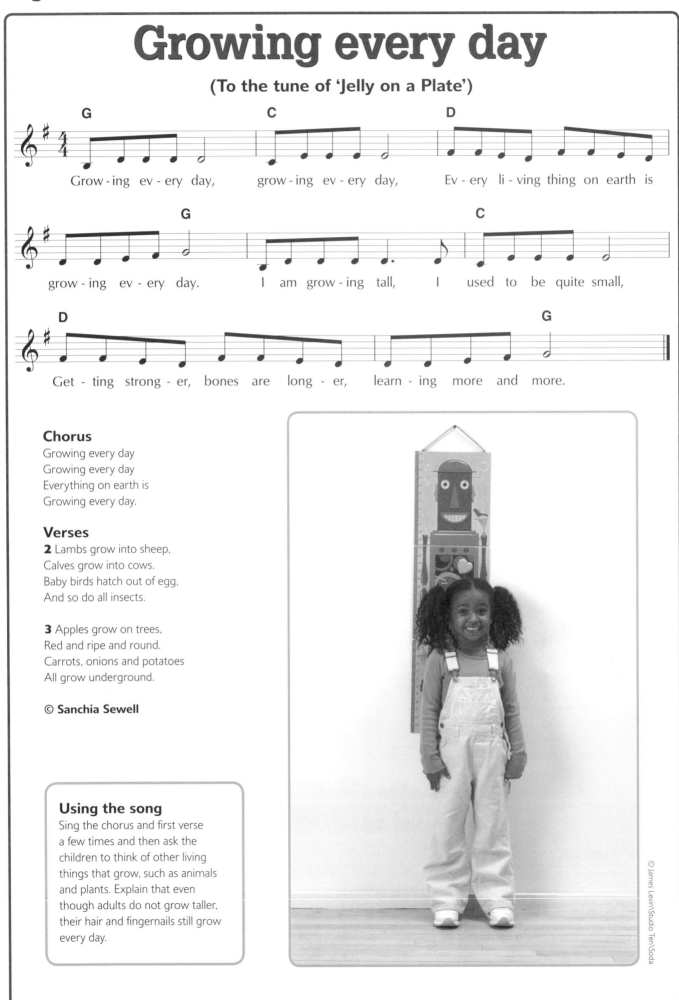

Grow - ing ev - ery day, grow - ing ev - ery day, Ev - ery li - ving thing on earth is

grow - ing ev - ery day. I am grow - ing tall, I used to be quite small,

Get - ting strong - er, bones are long - er, learn - ing more and more.

## Chorus

Growing every day
Growing every day
Everything on earth is
Growing every day.

## Verses

**2** Lambs grow into sheep,
Calves grow into cows.
Baby birds hatch out of egg,
And so do all insects.

**3** Apples grow on trees,
Red and ripe and round.
Carrots, onions and potatoes
All grow underground.

**© Sanchia Sewell**

### Using the song

Sing the chorus and first verse
a few times and then ask the
children to think of other living
things that grow, such as animals
and plants. Explain that even
though adults do not grow taller,
their hair and fingernails still grow
every day.

© James Levin\Studio Ten\Soda

# Daffodil, daffodil

## (Sung to the tune of 'This Old Man')

1. Daf-fo-dil, daf-fo-dil, Yel-low trum-pet tall and still, The __ daf-fo-dil tells me __ it's __ spring, Jump in the air and dance and sing.

**2** Snowdrop white, snowdrop white,
Tiny little flower bright,
The snowdrop tells me that it's spring,
Jump in the air and dance and sing.

**3** Crocus bright, crocus bright,
Purple, yellow, creamy white,
The crocus tells us that it's spring,
Jump in the air and dance and sing.

© **Johanne Levy**

### Using the song

Invite the children to stand in a circle.

Sing the first verse brightly, encouraging the children to pretend to be a daffodil standing as tall and still as possible. When they sing the fourth line, the children should jump on the word 'jump' and march on the spot when they sing 'dance and sing'.

Sing the second verse softly, almost whispered, to imply a shy, tiny flower just peeping out. Change the mood for the fourth line and repeat the actions as for the first verse.

Sing the third verse merrily and loudly, repeating the same actions as before for the fourth line.

© ImageState